Riding Tall in the Saddle

Riding Tall in the Saddle

The Cowboy Fact Book

Angel Vigil

2002

LIBRARIES UNLIMITED
Teacher Ideas Press
A Division of Greenwood Publishing Group, Inc.
Greenwood Village, Colorado

LIBRARIES UNLIMITED
Teacher Ideas Press
7730 East Belleview Avenue, Suite A200
Greenwood Village, CO 80111
1-800-225-5800
www.lu.com

Library of Congress Cataloging-in-Publication Data

Vigil, Angel.
  Riding tall in the saddle : the cowboy fact book / Angel Vigil.
    p. cm.
Includes bibliographical references and index.
    ISBN 1-56308-902-5
    1. Cowboys--West (U.S.)--History--Miscellanea. 2. Cowboys--West
(U.S.)--Social life and customs--Miscellanea. 3. West
(U.S.)--History--Miscellanea. 4. West (U.S.)--Social life and
customs--Miscellanea. I. Title.
    F596 .V54 2002
    978--dc21
                                                            2002004882

This book is dedicated to

Joe McLaughlin,

*a great Texas cowboy who rides tall
in the saddle and is definitely one to
ride the river with.*

Contents

Preface

One of my best childhood memories is an image I have of myself sitting in front of the television set—black and white only in those days—watching my hero, the Lone Ranger. First I would hear the thrilling and rushing notes of the William Tell Overture. Then those stirring, noble words:

> A fiery horse with the speed of light, a cloud of dust and a hearty "Hi Yo Silver!" The Lone Ranger. "Hi Yo Silver, away!" With his faithful Indian companion, Tonto, the daring and re-sourceful masked rider of the plains led the fight for law and order in the early west. Return with us now to those thrilling days of yesteryear. The Lone Ranger rides again.

As I watched each danger-filled episode, I eagerly anticipated the closing refrain of every show: "Who was that masked man?"

Rivaling the Lone Ranger in my boyhood cowboy pantheon was the ele-gantly attired Hispanic cowboy hero, the Cisco Kid, with his comic sidekick Pancho. The Cisco Kid actually had a job very similar to the Lone Ranger's. They both traveled the Old West, righting wrongs and fighting injustice wherever they found it. I still chuckle when I remember the closing words of comic affection that passed between Cisco and Pancho after they had once more vanquished the evil villains, saved the day, and brought to a close another excit-ing Cisco Kid episode: "Oh, Cisco!" "Oh, Pancho!"

I also remember a recurring joke between Cisco and Pancho that received a special nod of recognition in my own Hispanic family. Pancho would tell Cisco that they were having something different for supper instead of the usual beans and rice; they were having rice and beans! Now I laugh even more at myself as I remember how such a silly joke would bring laughter to my family.

Of course, what I am describing is my typical American boy's childhood of the 1950s and 1960s, a childhood filled with the exciting stories of the American cowboy. I faithfully and eagerly followed the adventures of my cowboy heroes through their television shows and comic books. To an American boy of the 1950s, the cowboy represented all that was exciting in life: heroism, bravery, vic-tory, and blazing guns. Their names ring out like a litany of boyhood saints: the

Lone Ranger, the Cisco Kid, Red Ryder, Roy Rogers, Zorro, Gene Autry, Gunsmoke's Matt Dillon, Hopalong Cassidy, Wyatt Earp, Wild Bill Hickok, and the many cowboy characters played by John Wayne. Finally, I cannot leave out that western wonder dog hero, working out of the legendary Fort Apache, Arizona Territory: Rin-Tin-Tin.

Standing with his father, the author is all decked out in his cowboy outfit with a black hat, fancy cowboy shirt, bandana, and pistol.

I further recall that in those politically incorrect days it was still all right to pass summer days playing cowboys and Indians. My imagination, fueled by the myth-making machinery of movies and television, created an active imaginary world in which I played out the exploits of my cowboy heroes. Like the longing boy in Jean Shepard's delightfully comic childhood memoir film, *The Christmas*

Story, all I really ever wanted as a child was my own Daisy Red Ryder BB gun. Then I would be a real cowboy, just like Red Ryder.

In addition to the typical cowboy play of my childhood, the world of the cowboy was constant in my life because I grew up in the American West, in New Mexico and Texas. I grew up listening to my mother recall fond memories of her daring exploits, riding her horse Croppy, her faithful childhood companion. A simple trip to my mother's home farm or a walk through my Texas hometown exposed me to the modern American cowboy, the working ranch hand. And no western childhood was complete without a trip to the rodeo.

As my childhood passed, my fascination with the cowboy faded. Living in the West, I was constantly aware of America's cowboy heritage, but it was no longer an active part of my own personal history. As I put away the things of childhood, the cowboy became a plaything of my past.

Now my story fast-forwards to my adulthood when the cowboy unexpectedly came riding back into my life. The re-awakening of my cowboy awareness began with my work as an author. Up to now, my books have focused on various aspects of Southwestern Hispanic culture. I write my books to help preserve and maintain the beautiful and proud aspects of Hispanic cultural heritage.

As part of my work as an author and *cuentista* (Hispanic storyteller), I often present storytelling shows on the traditional stories of the Hispanic Southwest and Mexico at schools and museums. At one museum, I was asked to develop a historical Hispanic character for an "old-time days" festival. After much research, I settled on the Spanish/Mexican cowboy, the *vaquero*. I found that studying the *vaquero* rekindled my fascination with the cowboy, and it dovetailed nicely with my interest in preserving and presenting important aspects of Hispanic culture.

I began my research for the *vaquero* character with the arrival of the Spanish, when they introduced cows, horses, and Spanish ranch culture and practices to the New World, and continued through the great cattle drives of the 1800s. I then continued to research how Hollywood established the American cowboy mythos and its current expression in modern western ranch and rodeo life.

The costumed historical re-enactment character I developed quickly grew into a show of its own, *Cuentos del Vaquero*, Stories of the *Vaquero*. The show became very popular in schools and museums. As Diego Martín, *el vaquero*, the Spanish colonial cowboy, I present western "living history." The show reveals a lost history, the immense role the Spanish/Mexican *vaquero* played in establishing western cattle and ranch culture. The *vaquero's* story tells the history of the origins and development of traditional cowboy practices in the American West.

In addition to my research for the show, I gathered an important amount of information on cowboy practices from ranch workers who would stand at the back of my shows and listen to my presentation, their arms folded in front of their chests, their faces revealing little. I rightly felt they were my truest test as to whether I had "gotten it right." After my very first show, one cowboy came up and shared his history with me and showed me how he threw a rope in comparison to my rope-throwing technique. This exchange became a model for many wonderful conversations I have had after my shows with ranch workers concerning the ways of the modern cowboy.

My editor at Libraries Unlimited became aware of my work on cowboys and suggested that I write a book for them; a simple but thorough fact book that would serve as an introduction to the history and world of cowboys. Many of their publications provide research support materials for schools and libraries, and they felt a book on cowboys would fill a research need. My own research on cowboy books for students revealed that they fell into two general categories. One category contained slight, but colorful books aimed at elementary students. The other category contained detailed books for more adult, academic-style research. My own school librarian pointed out the need for a book on cowboys directed at the young adult-level reader: a book filled with sufficient facts and depth to fulfill the research needs of middle school students.

So my journey as an author has returned me to my childhood world of cowboys. This time the world is not filled with a young boy's playful imaginings of bravery and smoking pistols. It is filled with a deep appreciation for the role the cowboy has played in American life, especially the settling and development of the American West. It is also filled with the direct memories of the many working ranch hands who have shared their lives with me.

Through my research on the cowboy, my historical re-enactment *vaquero* presentations, and my many conversations with working cowboys, I have come to understand why the cowboy myth was large enough to ignite a young boy's imagination. I also came to appreciate why the myth was important enough to stand at the center of a country's history and to support a country's self-image. I hope this book on cowboys will help explain the origins, development, and history of the most powerful and enduring American myth: the cowboy, on his horse, riding tall in the saddle, his self-reliant, independent spirit representing all that is good in the American character.

"Hi Yo Silver, away!"

Acknowledgments

I would like to thank my publisher, Libraries Unlimited, for its continued support of my work as an author. This is my fourth book for Libraries Unlimited, and I am proud to be one of their authors.

I also wish to thank my editor, Barbara Ittner. She gave me the opportunity to write this book, and she has been a constant source of advice and guidance.

I thank my long-time collaborator and friend, artist Carol Kimball. This is my fifth book with her, and I continue to be thankful that she has been willing to share her artistic talents on these projects. My books have always been better because of her wonderful spirit and amazing artistry.

I am especially thankful to all the research librarians who have given me such useful help in all my searches for just the right photo or reference material. The librarians of the Denver Western History/Genealogy Department of the Denver Public Library, the Colorado Historical Society, and the Buffalo Bill Historical Center deserve special thanks for the assistance they gave me on this project.

I also wish to thank my wife, Sheila, and my daughters, Tess and Sarah, for their support and consideration during the time I was writing this book.

Introduction

■ The creation of the myth

In his book *Californicos, The Saga of the Hard-riding Vaqueros, America's First Cowboys*, legendary western author and illustrator Jo Mora writes this nostalgic description of the cowboy:

> Here was the original native-son vaquero of our United States, another of those picturesque types that mushroomed to glory, did their bit in the building of our history, and then were properly labeled and stored away in the museum cabinet of our glorious Western Americana. (1994, 86)

A Mexican Buckaroo, by Frederic Remington, *Harper's Monthly*, July 1890.

Mora accurately describes the fate of the traditional "real" cowboy, the cowboy of the great trail drives. The cowboys of the 1800s were destined to disappear into the pages of American history and be replaced by a cowboy myth built by movies, television, and western literature.

Of course, the cowboy has not completely disappeared from American life. His image and myth are as vital as they ever were, sustained by the romanticized depictions of western music, American folklore, American popular culture, even modern ranch workers and rodeo stars. What has been lost, or put away in a museum as forgotten history as Mora describes, is the true story of the historical American cowboy, the trail drive cowboy, the story of his hard life, his challenging work, and his determined character.

The historical cowboy, from the early-era Spanish *vaquero* of the 1500s to the trail-drive cowboy of the 1800s, is the source for the mythical cowboy. The dime pulp novel cowboy, the Hollywood cowboy, the television cowboy, and the rodeo cowboy all owe their existence to the forgotten trail-drive cowboy.

The transformation of the historical cowboy into the mythical cowboy is in itself a story of the West. This transformation occurred over several generations, but once it was completed, America had created its most powerful and enduring myth: the American cowboy. This transformation had many contributors. Each contributor added his own layering to the myth, and each contributed to the myth's development and refinement.

Early western illustrators created the first images of cowboy life for the American public. Frederic Remington, Charles Russell, and Charles Siringo each painted the cowboy's life accurately and realistically. Americans saw these pictures and imagined the wonderful life of the western cowboy. People who had never traveled to the West had clear images of the cowboy's life. These illustrations were the beginning of the myth. In a time before television and movies, these images and their wide distribution in publications such as *Harper's Weekly* gave Americans their first impression of cowboy life.

Americans soon learned more about cowboy life through the dime pulp novels of the late 1800s and early 1900s. These novels presented a heavily fictionalized version of cowboy life filled with daring adventures, racing stagecoaches, super-hero cowboys, and blazing gun battles with villains. These exaggerated stories inflamed the American public's imagination and created romanticized images that had little in common with the daily realities of the working cowboy. For many people, however, these novels were the only stories of cowboys they read, and they presented such an attractive image that the truth paled in comparison.

A detail from a classic Frederic Remington painting: a cowboy riding hard across the prairie, fighting a prairie fire by pulling the hide of a freshly killed steer across the flames. He learned this fire-fighting technique from the Indians, who used buffalo hides the same way. *Harper's Weekly*, October 27, 1888.

Stella, the Girl Range Rider. Cover of *Rough Rider Weekly.* "She had snatched the blacksnake from Old Dennis as she passed the grub-wagon. Now she laid it into the stampeding herd with vicious strokes. Would she turn them in time?" September 1, 1906.

The Wild West Shows, as popularized by Buffalo Bill Cody and his cohorts, gave American and European audiences theatrical presentations of the cowboy myth. Through these elaborately produced shows, audiences saw yet another romanticized version of the cowboy. Even though they were theatrical spectacles, audiences saw them as historical truth. Including native Indians such as Chief Sitting Bull gave the perception of historical accuracy. For many audiences, these shows taught them all they knew about the cowboy history of the West.

Western literature, from the early novels of Zane Grey, who published his first book in 1913—the famous *Riders of the Purple Sage*—to the modern writer Louis L'Amour, who has published more than 100 western novels, also contributed immensely to the development of the mythical cowboy. These novels added to the literary clichés first employed by the pulp novels: dangerous adventure; wily rustlers and villains; innocent womanhood; and brave, stoic, and heroic cowboys.

The development of the rodeo added another layer to the myth. When the trail drives ended, the cowboys were out of work. So they created the rodeo, modeled after the cowboy contests they had seen the Mexican *vaqueros* perform, as an alternative arena in which they could still display their skills.

Both men and women competed in the early rodeos. At first, the rodeos were no more than gatherings in an open field where cowboys and cowgirls would compete and show off their skills. These rodeos, with their daring displays of skill, added to the wild and reckless, but highly skilled, image of the American cowboy.

Edgar Bobbit on Canahejo, First Money, Steamboat Springs.

Finally, Hollywood movies, and later, radio and television shows, built upon these fabricated cowboy images and created even stronger and more fanciful images. Through the vast power of the entertainment industry, the romanticized myth of the American cowboy was completed and spread throughout the world.

The "B" movies of the 1930s, the action movies of the 1940s and 1950s, and the television series of the 1950s and 1960s gave the world such cowboy heroes as Tom Mix, Roy Rogers, Gene Autry, Hopalong Cassidy, Annie Oakley, the Cisco Kid, the Lone Ranger, and John Wayne.

Television enhanced the myth with its weekly presentations of cowboy heroism and western adventures. Television shows such as *The Lone Ranger, The Roy Rogers Show, Gunsmoke, Have Gun Will Travel, The Rifleman, Maverick, Rawhide, Death Valley Days,* and *Bonanza* saturated American popular culture with powerful images of larger-than-life cowboy heroes. More recently, the *Lonesome Dove* television series continued America's fascination with the cowboy story.

Cowboy heroes as presented in movies and television, whether as dandified as the singing cowboys, as brave as the justice-seeking cowboy, or as tough as the two-fisted barroom brawlers and gunslingers, became America's heroes. Their influence is best expressed in the words of singing legend Willie Nelson's lyrics: "My heroes have always been cowboys."

The hero Willie Nelson sings about is, of course, the true-blue American cowboy hero; the mythical hero created by American popular culture and the entertainment industry. Although the true cowboy of the great trail drives is lost to history, his glory lives on in the greatness of the mythical American cowboy: a cowboy alone on the range, independent, proud, and riding tall in the saddle.

American cowboy riding tall in the saddle.

■ The purpose and organization of this book

The purpose of this book is to present the source of the American cowboy myth, the historical American cowboy, the trail-drive cowboy of the 1800s, who lived behind the legend. The book presents the development of cowboy and cattle culture from the days of the Spanish colonial *vaqueros* to the days of the trail-drive cowboy. The book's primary focus is to describe the era of the trail-drive cowboy—the "real" American cowboy. It is intended to guide the reader from the early history of the establishment of cowboy culture in the New World by the Spanish to the days of the great trail drives.

The book uses a question-and-answer format to present its information. I chose this format because I have experienced its success in other educational books. The format allows the reader to quickly and easily find the answers to questions about the subject being studied. It also allows the information to be presented in an efficient, concise, and organized manner.

In his book *The Cowboy Handbook*, Bruce Dillman quotes western writer J. Frank Dobie as saying, "Good Lord! Another book about cowboys? What on earth for?" Even though Dillman reports the quote in mock jest, Dobie does express a true sentiment.

This book answers Dobie's question in two ways. First, its format is unique in that its question-and-answer style is a useful and productive format seldom used in books. Second, the book fills a gap in the educational books about cowboys. Most books fall into two categories. Either they are very short books aimed at the elementary school level of reader, or they are academic books written for adults, scholars and researchers, and advanced students. This book fills a middle level between these two positions.

The book uses an abundance of historical photographs and accurate illustrations to enhance the text, which presents in-depth information on the most important cowboy topics. Aware of the present educational identification of different learning styles, I decided to include many additional photographs and illustrations to help the visual learner who needs support grasping the information in the written text.

The book targets the upper elementary and middle school student who needs more information than that presented at the elementary level, but does not require college-level information. The book also targets the adult reader who has a generalist level of curiosity about cowboys and seeks an easy-reading book with sufficient information to satisfy his or her search for answers to questions about cowboys and American cattle culture.

The book's chapters organize the material into six broad subject areas. Chapter 1, **At the Head of the Trail: The Beginnings of Cowboy Culture in the American West**, presents the origins of many different aspects of cowboy and cattle culture. The chapter examines the historical origins of the most important cowboy practices. It begins with the Spanish-era establishment of cattle culture in the New World and gives special attention to the importance of the often-ignored Spanish and Mexican founding contributions to American cowboy culture.

Chapter 2, **Tools of the Trade: I Can Tell by Your Outfit That You're a Cowboy**, gives in-depth descriptions of the working cowboy's clothing and tools as well as their historical origins.

Chapter 3, **The Great Trail Drives: The Glory Days of the Cowboy**, forms the heart of the book. The chapter covers the trail drives of the 1860s to the 1880s in detail. It also covers both the origins of the trail drives and their working practices. The daily work of the trail-drive cowboys, the role of the horses they used, and the cattle they drove to market are described. The goal of this chapter is to give the reader clear and true descriptions of the trail-drive cowboy's daily world.

Chapter 4, **Riding into the Sunset: The End of the Trail for the Cowboy**, covers the end of the trail drives. The chapter places their demise in a proper historical context and describes the fate of the trail-drive cowboy.

Chapter 5, **Cowboy Wisdom: Expert Facts About Cowboys**, is a collection of miscellaneous and fascinating facts. It presents the origins and definitions of cowboy words and slang, biographical portraits of important cowboys and cowgirls, and a historical timeline. It also presents an interesting review of the historical cowboy code of honor as well as the codes of honor written by movie and television cowboy heroes.

Chapter 6, **Happy Trails to You: Places to Go and Things to Do to Learn More About Cowboys**, is a guide to additional information sources about cowboys and cowboy life. It includes listings of Internet sites, great cowboy movies, and dude ranches.

At the Head of the Trail

The Beginnings of Cowboy Culture in the American West

◘ **Where did the word *cowboy* come from?**

One of the earliest known instances of the word *cowboy* being used was in Ireland around A.D. 1000. In those ancient days, the word actually was two words: *cow-boy* and referred to horsemen and cattle workers.

Another early use of the word *cow-boy* was in England in the 1620s. In this appearance, it referred to a young boy who herded cattle. During this period, the word *boy* meant a male house servant, so a cow-boy was a young male servant whose job was to herd cattle.

When colonizing America, the British, in order to increase the colonies' population, gave out-of-favor Irish cow-boys two choices: jail or America. Most chose America, where they worked as indentured servants to American farmers.

1

In early colonial America, the word *cow-boy* had a negative meaning. Men and boys raising and working with cattle called themselves cow herders or drovers. They did not call themselves cow-boys because of the negative association with the Irish indentured servant cow-boys.

During the American Revolution, the word *cow-boy* referred to British loyalists who stole American cattle and sold them to the British military forces. Another use of the word during this period referred to guerrilla Tory bands that hid in bushes and lured American patriots into ambush by ringing cowbells. Clearly, this version of the word's use during the American Revolution was very negative.

In the 1830s, Colonel John S. "Rip" Ford used the term to describe Texas border bandits who drove off Mexican cattle. The word was not considered as negative as it had been during the American Revolution because Texas was at war with Mexico, and their actions were considered patriotic to Texas. Still, even then, the term *cow-boy* referred to a cattle rustler.

From the 1830s to the 1860s in Texas, the word *vaquero* was commonly used to describe a cattle worker. Even during the era of the great American trail drives, men working with cattle were called by many names other than cow-boy; for example, drovers, punchers, or cow herders.

It was not until the 1880s that writers began referring to cattle workers as cow-boys. In his book *Cowboy Culture*, David Dary writes that in 1874, Joseph McCoy (the "father of the cow town" who established Abilene as the first railroad cow town) wrote: "We will here say for the benefit of our northern readers that . . . the ordinary laborer is termed a 'cow-boy.' " Richard Slatta, in his book *Cowboys of the Americas*, records that in 1883, a writer for the *Denver Republican* wrote "it matters not what age, if a man works on a salary and rides herd, he is called a 'cowboy.' "

By the 1900s, the hyphen had been dropped, and cowboy became the universal name for anybody who worked with cattle in the American West.

■ What were some other names for cowboys?

There were many other names for cowboys, including drover, cowpuncher, puncher, waddie, cattleman, *vaquero*, buckaroo, and wrangler.

- ★ Drover came from the cowboys who drove the cattle to market on the trail drives.
- ★ Cowpuncher or puncher originated from the cowboys who used long poles to punch or prod cows into the railroad cars at the railhead.

★ Waddie came from the cowboy word "wad," meaning something that fills in, just as a man would fill in and complete a trail drive outfit.

★ *Vaquero* was the Spanish name for a person who worked with cattle. *Vaca* is the Spanish word for cow.

★ Buckaroo comes from the Spanish word *vaquero.*

★ Wrangler comes from the Spanish word *caballerango,* meaning a stableman or horse trainer.

▓ How did cows and horses get to America?

Scientists believe that primitive ancestors of the modern horse existed in the Americas tens of millions of years ago, but these early horses did not survive. When the Spanish arrived, there were no cows or horses in the New World.

When the Spanish came to the New World, they brought all aspects of their culture with them: their language, their government, their stories, their food, their religion, and, of course, their animals. The origins of the Spanish horse can be traced back to when the Moors brought Arab horses into Spain when they invaded in A.D 711. The Spanish also had raised and worked cattle on their vast open plains for centuries, developing many of their cattle practices during the centuries-long Moorish occupation.

In 1494, on his second voyage to the New World, Christopher Columbus brought the hardy Andalusian "black cattle" to the Caribbean island he called Española, today the Dominican Republic and Haiti. He also unloaded 24 stallions and 10 mares, thus introducing cattle and Spanish ranching practices to the New World.

In 1521, Gregorio de Villalobos transported calves from the Caribbean islands to mainland Mexico, the first cows on the mainland New World continent. The Spanish brought three types of cattle to the New World: (1) the *Berrenda*, white cattle with black markings around the head and neck; (2) the *Retinto*, cattle with long, narrow heads and tan to cherry-red coloring; and (3) the *Ganado Prieto*, the black Andalusian fighting bull. These bulls were named for the region in southern Spain where the cattle originated.

In 1519, on his second trip to the New World, conquistador Hernán Cortés brought with him the legendary 16 horses—11 Andalusian stallions and 5 mares—thereby re-introducing the horse to the New World. Within a few centuries, these 16 horses would populate the Americas with vast numbers of wild horses.

■ Who were the first cowboys?

The first cowboys were native Indians of New Spain who tended to the vast cattle herds on the Spanish missions. To understand how the Indians became the first cowboys, it is necessary to understand a little bit about Spanish society and history in the New World.

Spanish society was complex and strict in its social hierarchy. A descriptive system of bloodline categories created strict classes within Spanish society. *Peninsulares* were pure Spaniards born in Spain, *criollos* were pure Spaniards born in the New World, *mestizos* were mixed Indian and Spanish, *mulatos* were mixed Black and Spanish, and *zambos* were mixed Black and Indian. During the colonial period, the greatest discrimination, after *Indios* (or Indians) and Blacks, fell on the people with the *mestizo* or *zambo* bloodline.

The result of this class system, based upon birthplace and family heritage, was that the native Indians were at the bottom of the social hierarchy. In turn, this also meant that they were at the bottom of the labor pool and given the most difficult and undesirable work. In truth, many Indians worked in near slavery.

In addition to the immense task of establishing New Spain, the Spanish also continued their vast exploration of the New World. While Spaniards explored both North and South America, we are most concerned with the northern outposts of the Spanish empire. In 1539, explorer Francisco Vásquez de Coronado, under orders from the Viceroys of New Spain, entered the northern frontier of New Spain searching for the legendary Seven Cities of Gold. His search was futile, but his explorations established the northern frontiers of New Spain for colonizing expeditions.

In 1598, Don Juan de Oñate led the first expedition to succeed in establishing a permanent colony in New Mexico, along the Upper Rio Grande Valley. Soon after, the clergy and military followed, further colonizing the northern frontier of New Spain.

In their great effort to establish their culture in the New World, the Spanish sent missionaries to the New World determined to convert the native people to Roman Catholic Christianity. They established missions dedicated to educating the native converts and teaching them the Spanish religion, language, and culture. A very important settlement path was along the coast of the northwestern frontier. Father Junípero Serra was a Franciscan missionary in California during the 1700s. He was instrumental in founding 21 missions in California along *el Camino Real* (the Royal Highway), a road connecting all the missions along the California coast, from San Diego to San Francisco.

In Arizona, Father Kino established stock ranches in many locations in the Santa Cruz Valley. Father Kino believed that tending cattle was an important part of converting and supporting the Arizona Indians.

Soldier–herd driver with Oñate, 1598. The soldiers had the dual role of maintaining the caravan's safety as well as herding the animals. The soldier carries an iron-tipped lance, the *desjarretadera*. The lance was 10–12 feet long. The soldier used it like a jousting pole to drive cattle to their destination and to hamstring cattle selected for slaughter for hides and tallow.

Through the decades following the establishment of New Spain, the Spaniards founded many missions and military settlements, followed by civilian settlements. As these civilian settlements expanded throughout the northern frontiers of New Spain, they helped consolidate Spanish culture in the New World.

Now, after this brief examination of the Spaniards' world, their class society and far-reaching exploration and settlement, we can begin to search for the roots of the first cowboy in the Americas.

When first colonizing what came to be known as New Spain, the Spanish found the land and climate of the New World perfect for raising their cattle. The large open plains of Mexico, the ample grasslands, the favorable climate, and the lack of predators allowed both the cattle and horses to roam freely and multiply quickly. The Spanish developed their vast cattle herds in the area encompassing western central Mexico.

Every expedition that left to explore and settle the New World took Spanish cattle and horses along. Soon the Spanish cattle empire stretched from the interior of Mexico all the way to what eventually became California and the southwestern United States.

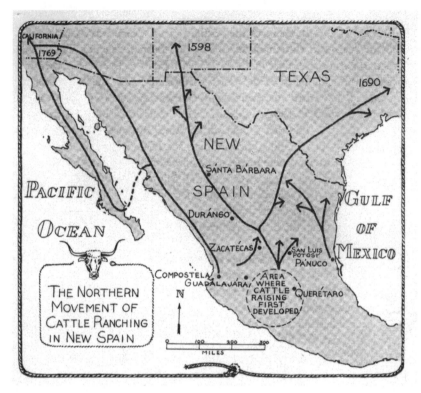

The northern movement of cattle ranching in New Spain.

The Spanish had created a difficult dilemma for themselves with respect to their far-flung cattle empire. On one hand, no Spanish gentleman or missionary would ever do the difficult, dangerous, and dirty job of working cattle herds. On the other hand, since they viewed the horse as an animal of domination and control over the native populations, they had passed a law stating that no native Indian was allowed to own or ride a horse. The crux of the dilemma is simply stated: If Spanish gentlemen or missionaries would not tend to the cows because such work was below their station in Spanish society, and if the Indians were not allowed to ride horses, then who was to do the hard work of managing cattle?

The answer was simple: the native Indians. The native Indians, because of their low position in Spanish society, were the only people available for the challenging work of tending to cattle herds. Spanish missionaries, especially in the California missions, disobeyed the law out of necessity and taught Indians how to ride horses and how to work the cattle herds.

Since the horse population had grown so explosively, wild horses ran loose throughout the empire of New Spain. In a short time, Indians managed to capture their own horses and became expert horse riders. With their horse-riding skills and the cattle knowledge taught to them by the Spanish missionaries, native Indians became the first cowboys in the New World who inherited the centuries-old Spanish knowledge, skills, and techniques for managing large herds of cattle with horses on the open range. The native Indians were the first *vaqueros* of the New World.

Mission Indian *vaquero.*

■ What is a *vaquero*?

The word *vaquero* means "one who works with cows." It is not the Spanish word for "cowboy." *Vaquero* is a combination of two Spanish words. The word *vaca* means cow. Also, the word ending of *ero* always signifies and identifies that a person is involved in the named activity. So, the word *vaquero* simply means "one who works with cows."

Vaqueros were the first cowboys. As described in the preceding section, at first they were native Indians who had been taught how to ride horses and manage the cattle herds by the Spanish missionaries. Later, *vaqueros* were Mexican *mestizos,* men of mixed Spanish and Indian heritage, who were hired to tend to the cattle herds of colonial Mexico. Over time the word *vaquero* came to mean any man who worked with cattle. In Texas in the 1830s to 1860s, *vaquero* was used for any man working cattle, regardless of the man's ethnic heritage.

■ Where did the first ranches come from?

Ranching first began in Spain in the eleventh century. People throughout Europe tended small herds of cattle for food, milk, and leather. However, on the Andalusian Plains, the Spanish developed techniques and equipment for herding hundreds and thousands of cattle on open ranges. This Spanish ranching culture was the foundation of the first American ranches.

The first *ranchos*, or ranches, in the Southwest were Mexican in origin. These first ranches were the result of two Spanish settlement systems in the northern frontiers of New Spain. The first settlement system was the mission system. Missionaries from Spain came to the New World determined to convert the native people to Roman Catholic Christianity. They built missions dedicated to educating the native converts and teaching them the Spanish religion, language, and culture. While the Spanish established missions throughout the Southwest, the missions in California and Texas were the most important for creating a cattle and ranch culture.

Father Junípero Serra was a Franciscan missionary in California during the 1700s. Beginning in 1769, he was instrumental in founding 21 missions in California along *el Camino Real* (the Royal Highway), a road connecting all the missions along the California coast, from San Diego to San Francisco. In Texas, the Spanish began their mission system by establishing the first mission and presidio at San Antonio in 1718. By 1770, as many as 4,000 head of cattle were being herded near San Antonio.

The second important settlement system was the Spanish land-grant system, the *encomienda*. Through this system, the Spanish granted ownership of large parcels of land in the Southwest to Spanish court officers and gentlemen. These land grants became the foundation of the large Spanish *haciendas*, the first ranches of the Southwest. The owners of these land grants were called *hacendados* or *rancheros*.

In both of these settlements, the missions and the *haciendas*, the Spanish had cattle and horses. Wherever the Spanish built settlements, they brought stock herds with them. They also brought the *vaqueros* to work with the cattle and horses. This mission and land-grant system produced huge cattle herds. By the time the Pilgrims had landed on Plymouth Rock, Spanish *hacendados* were branding 30,000 calves a year on their *ranchos,* and they claimed herds in the tens of thousands.

South Texas *ranchero*, circa 1815. His ornate clothing and horse's gear imitated the clothing of Spanish noblemen.

This combination of mission lands and *hacienda* settlements, *vaqueros* to work the herds, and the Spanish cattle culture was the foundation of the first ranches in the Southwest.

■ How did the first Texans learn about herding cattle?

The area in south Texas between the Rio Grande River and the Nueces River, roughly between San Antonio and Brownsville, has been called the "cradle of cattle culture." This area was the source of the large Texas cattle kingdoms and the great trail drives. It also was the birthplace of the Texas cowboy. On some old maps, this area of Texas was marked as "Wild Horse Country."

To understand why this area was the center of cattle culture and how the Texas cowboy came into existence, one must first know a little bit about the history between Texas and Mexico. Texas has had a complicated historical relationship with Mexico. For more than 200 years, the Texas territory was part of New Spain and then Mexico. Mexico owned and controlled the Texas territory.

During this time, literally millions of Mexican cattle roamed the Texas plains, and Mexican *vaqueros* worked on the large *haciendas* of colonial Mexico.

In 1836, after several intense battles with the Mexican government, including the Battle of the Alamo, Texas declared itself an independent nation. Shortly afterward, in 1848, Mexico lost a war with the United States, and, as part of a huge land settlement that saw Mexico lose over half its territory, Texas officially became part of the United States.

During the period leading up to its battles with Texas, the Mexican government had approved American settlement in Texas. During the early part of the 1800s, American settlers poured into Texas. In 1821, Stephen F. Austin received permission from the Mexican government to settle an American colony in the San Antonio valley. Many of these settlers came from the eastern and southern parts of the United States. When these settlers first encountered the large, free-roaming herds in Texas, they thought the cattle belonged to no one, so they rounded up the longhorns for hides, tallow, and horns. To the Mexicans, these Texans were cattle thieves and this added controversy to the tension brewing between the Texans and Mexicans.

These English-speaking settlers were really cow herders who were used to moving small herds of cattle to and from local pastures. They had never encountered thousands and thousands of wild longhorn cows roaming freely on the vast open plains of Texas and didn't know how to manage so many cows on such large lands.

The Spanish colonial, and later Mexican, *vaqueros* living and working in Texas at the time, however, were experts at managing the longhorn Texas cattle. For centuries they had been transplanting Spanish cattle practices to the New World and by the 1800s had firmly established a well-developed cattle culture in what would soon become the southwestern part of the United States.

The *vaqueros* introduced the Anglo-American Texas settlers to the cattle business and shared with them their extraordinary skills in horsemanship and cattle management. The Anglo-American Texans quickly adopted all aspects of Spanish cattle culture. Every part of Texan cattle culture, from cowboy dress, language, horse equipment, techniques of cattle roundups and branding, and herd management, came from the *vaqueros*. After Texas became a state, ranchers would hire Mexican *vaqueros* to work on their ranches. In this way, Mexican *vaqueros* continued to teach Texas cowboys and influence the development of Texan cattle culture.

■ How did the Indians become such expert horsemen?

When the Spanish arrived in the New World, there were no horses. They brought their horses with them, introducing them to America.

When the native Indians first saw the Spanish riding their horses, they mistakenly believed they were seeing an unimaginable creature, a combination of man and beast. Soon they discovered that the man and beast were separate.

The Spanish viewed the horse as an animal of dominance. In fact, many historians credit the horse with being part of the reason the Spanish were able to establish dominance over the native populations so quickly. Because the horse was so important in their control over the native populations, the Spanish passed laws stating that it was illegal for any native Indian to own or ride a horse.

As stated earlier, the Spanish soon came to need the native population to tend and manage their large cattle herds. Spanish missionaries were the first to train native Indians in how to ride horses and use them to manage the cattle herds. Soon, the *hacienda* owners also began to hire native Indians to manage their cattle herds. By the 1600s and 1700s, the herds had become larger and more difficult to manage. *Mestizo*, or mixed-blood, Indians and the "Christianized" Indians were soon doing all the work of managing the Spanish cattle herds. Within a few generations, the native Indians had become horse experts. By 1650, Indians, especially the Apache and the Comanche, had become master horsemen on their own.

As was inevitable, many horses escaped from the missions and ranches and formed wild herds of horses that roamed freely. The native Indians were able to capture these horses and train them for their own uses. Horses captured by the Indians later became the stock horses for the Plains Indians, whose prowess with horses played an important role in their battles with American settlers and the military in the 1800s.

In just a few generations, the Southwest had both millions of wild horses and native Indians who were expert in capturing, training, and using them.

■ What was the original use of cattle before the days of the great trail drives?

Cattle have always been a source of food. The Spanish and Mexicans who established the cattle culture in the New World and the American Southwest used cattle for food; this was the first and most direct use of cattle. However, there were far more cows available than they needed to supply their food needs.

These surplus cattle were more than enough to support a second business dependent upon cattle.

Cattle were also used for hide and tallow. Cattle hide, of course, was used for leather clothing and leather goods. Tallow, or animal fat, was used for making such goods as candles, soaps, and lubricants. In California, many of the *vaqueros* worked for hide and tallow companies. Sea traders and shipping companies would call on California ports to buy and barter for leather and tallow. Sailors began calling cattle hides "California bank notes." As early as 1598, a fleet of ships transported 150,000 hides to Spain.

One of the reasons cattle were so cheap—indeed almost worthless—was that there were so many running loose on the open ranges and the Spanish and Mexicans used all they needed for food and the hide and tallow business. People in the eastern United States also needed cattle and their by-products, but there was no way to easily and economically transport the cattle to them. When the railroad finally provided a solution to the cattle transportation problem, the era of the great trail drives began.

■ How did the Spanish cow turn into the Texas longhorn?

The mighty Texas longhorn descends from the cattle the Spanish brought to the New World. As mentioned previously, the Spanish brought three types of cows with them: (1) the *Berrenda*, (2) the *Retinto*, and (3) the *Ganado Prieto*. The

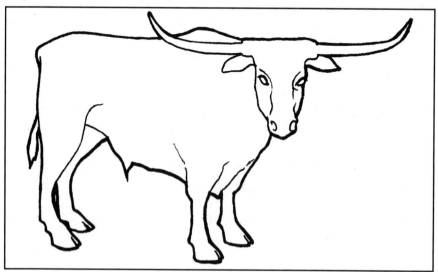

The Texas longhorn.

English brought the Durham and Hereford cow descended from English stock. Cross-breeding the Spanish cattle, primarily the *Retinto*, with the English cattle produced the Texas longhorn.

■ Why was the longhorn cow such a perfect cow for the cattle drives?

The remarkable and legendary Texas longhorn was perfectly adapted to the rigors of the trail drive. Its horns grew up to 6 feet long, with the largest measuring 8 feet. Its sway-backed body was narrow and lanky and weighed almost a ton. Hardy and long legged, it could cover long distances. It thrived on the high, semi-arid, timberless grasslands that were very similar to the Spanish plains they had originally been bred on. The longhorn was renowned for its mean and temperamental disposition, a result of its ancestry with the Spanish fighting bull.

The trail drives were harsh experiences for cattle. Marching over very long distances with very little food and water, in unpredictable weather, and subject to many dangers, only a breed as tough and durable as the longhorn could survive the trail and still produce a profit for the owner upon its sale at the railroad stockyards.

■ What type of horse was used on the cattle drives?

When the Spanish reintroduced the horse to the New World, they brought Spanish Arabian horses with them. These horses were the product of generations of breeding between Spanish horses and the Arab horses of the Moors. These Spanish-Arabian horses became the ancestors of the wild mustangs that roamed the Southwest in large herds just before the trail drives.

These wild mustangs were small horses, weighing between 600 and 800 pounds. The Spanish *vaqueros* and the Anglo settlers captured,

Frederic Remington illustration of a cowboy herding wild mustangs.

broke, and trained these wild mustangs to be cow horses for ranch work and, later, the trail drives.

The most popular horse for ranch work was the quarter horse. The quarter horse was the first American breed selectively bred for specific traits. Cattlemen bred the Spanish horse and the English thoroughbreds to produce a small, agile horse capable of short, intense bursts of speed. Its sure-footed speed allowed it to catch cattle and respond quickly to the commands of the cowboy ranch worker and trail driver. Like its cattle counterpart, the longhorn, the quarter horse was the perfect animal for the hard specific work of the ranch and the trail drive.

■ How did the rodeo start?

The rodeo, as the modern American cowboy practices it, is an exhibition of horsemanship combined with skill contests based upon traditional cowboy work. Both the word *rodeo* and the activities of the rodeo are descended from the early cattle hunts and games of the Spanish *vaqueros*.

The word *rodeo* is derived from the Spanish word *rodear*, which means "to surround" or "to gather." The first Spanish *rodeos* were cattle hunts or roundups during which the *vaqueros* would gather open-range cattle for branding. These Spanish *rodeos* were first organized for branding stock, but evolved to include other activities. The *rodeos* throughout the Southwest eventually developed into festive occasions with elaborate meals, music, and dancing.

A RODEO.

Old Mexico illustration of a rodeo, a Mexican cattle roundup, 1883.

The *vaqueros* also developed contests based upon their horsemanship skills. These games included activities such as the ring game: a contest in which *vaqueros* raced with a wooden lance at a suspended, small, gold ring. The rider who put his lance through the gold ring first was the winner. Another contest had riders jousting with canes. *Vaqueros* also engaged in exhibitions fighting bulls with long lances.

In another bull-related game—the *colear*—a rider raced alongside a bull, grabbed its tail, and twisted the tail around the saddle horn. He then quickly swerved to the side with his horse and spun the bull to the ground.

The *paso de la muerte*, or ride of death, was an especially dangerous game. In this game, a rider raced alongside a wild mustang. When he was right next to the horse, he leapt onto its back and rode it until he was thrown or the horse gave up.

The game of *rayar* involved two riders racing toward each other with a line drawn in the dirt between them. When the riders approached the line, they pulled back on the reins and reined the horse to a sudden stop. The rider who stopped closest to the line was the winner.

Another game had *vaqueros* place two coins between their knees and the saddle. They then raced around an obstacle course; the rider who finished the race first and still had the coins in place was the winner.

Other *vaquero* contests involved horse races, roping contests, and recreational displays of everyday *vaquero* cattle and horse skills. The skills the *vaqueros*

COWBOY RACE ON THE WESTERN PRAIRIES

Cowboy race on the western prairie.

exhibited during these large roundups also included bull riding, steer wrestling, and bucking horse riding.

When the Anglo settlers first witnessed the large Spanish *rodeos,* they also witnessed the *vaquero* games of skill. In time, the Anglo settlers appropriated the word *rodeo* and changed its meaning from the original term for a Spanish cattle gathering to its modern name for a cowboy contest involving cattle and horse skills.

The modern version of the rodeo first appeared at trail-drive gatherings at cow town corrals where trail-drive cowboys competed to see who was the top hand at riding and roping. Later, the Wild West Shows featured cowboy and Indian circuses, with demonstrations of sharpshooting, roping, and horsemanship.

Many towns claim to be the site of the first organized rodeo. No matter which town really wins this contested title, one fact is certain: By the 1880s, these cowboy rodeos had become common throughout the Southwest.

In 1869, in Deer Trail, Colorado, cowboys held what is considered to be the first organized, public cowboy contest in America. Held on the Fourth of July, the rodeo was the ancestor of today's modern American rodeo.

Prescott, Arizona, claims it started the rodeo in 1888. Prescott has the unique support of the Trivial Pursuit® game. The answer to the question, "What rough-and-tumble Western sport was first formalized in Prescott, Arizona?" is "rodeo."

The *Encyclopaedia Britannica* states that Denver, Colorado, was the site of the first paid spectator rodeo in 1887. The oldest and longest running annual show is Cheyenne Frontier Days, started in 1897.

By the early 1900s, rodeos were established as both cowboy skill contests and western entertainment and had become substitutes for real cowboy work. At this time, women competed equally with men, and many women became rodeo champions. By the 1930s, women's roles in the rodeo had been reduced to rodeo queens and barrel racing. This period of women's involvement and their successes in the rodeo is covered more thoroughly in the books by Judy Crandall, Mary LeCompte, and Joyce Gibson Roach listed in the Suggested Readings section at the end of this book. By the 1940s, the rodeo had developed into the form we now recognize as the modern American rodeo.

Mabel Strickland on "Stranger."

Mryme Stroud, trick-riding belle.

■ How did the Mexican *charro* begin?

The word *charro* became associated with horsemen in the late eighteenth century. Spanish horsemen began to decorate their clothing and horse gear with silver buttons, fringe, and other decorative accessories. Common people described this fancy attire as being "*charro*," a Spanish word meaning gaudy, showy, loud, and overly fancy. Over time, the term lost its derogatory inference and became a reference to a positive representation of the enduring ideals of the proud and valiant Mexican horseman.

The Mexican *charro* is based upon the legacy of the *caballero*, the Spanish gentleman rider. During the period of Spanish-colonial Mexico, from the 1500s through the 1800s, the Spanish elite included gentlemen riders—riders who rode proud, beautiful horses and who wore richly ornate clothing while riding. These Spanish elite received land grants, *encomiendas*, from the Spanish government. These land grants became the foundations of the *ranchos* or *haciendas*, large Mexican ranches dedicated to the business of horses and cattle. In time, the *caballeros* also became known as *hacendados*, the gentleman ranchers and owners of the *haciendas*.

These wealthy *hacendados* became known for their rich dress and excellent horsemanship. Their style of dress, featuring richly decorated jackets and pants, became the basis for the modern *charro* outfit. This fancy *charro* dress reflected the wealth and status of the gentlemen riders.

In the 1880s, Mexico City began hosting early exhibitions of *charro* riding. These exhibitions grew in frequency and popularity until the Mexican Revolution in 1910. After the Mexican Revolution, the horse and stock supply decreased in Mexico, and the *charro* diminished in importance.

In 1921, a Tamaulipas lawyer named Ramón Cosío Gonzalés organized the National Association of Charros and began *charreadas*, organized exhibitions of riding and horsemanship. His efforts began a renaissance of the *charro* experience, and the *charro* once again became an important Mexican figure. This renaissance of the *charro* has continued to the present day, and the *charro* has become one of Mexico's primary and most important cultural figures.

Tools of the Trade

I Can Tell by Your Outfit That You're a Cowboy

■ What was the cowboy outfit?

In cowboy talk, the cowboy "outfit" refers to the work clothes and items the cowboy uses when he is working with cattle. The Spanish and Mexican *vaqueros* developed the original cowboy outfit. When the Anglo settlers were adapting to the cattle and ranch culture of the *vaqueros,* they were influenced by the *vaqueros* about what type of clothes to wear when herding cattle on the open plains. The Anglo cowboy took the basic elements of the *vaquero* outfit and developed a very defined set of clothes that served only one purpose: protecting the cowboy while he was working with cattle. The standard look for the cowboy outfit included the following items: a wide-brimmed hat, a bandana, wool or denim pants, a vest, chaps, boots, spurs, a saddle, a seldom worn Colt .44 or .45 six-gun, a cotton or flannel shirt, gloves, and gauntlets (leather forearm guards). Cowboys wore gauntlets, or cuffs, on their forearms for additional protection when riding through rough brush.

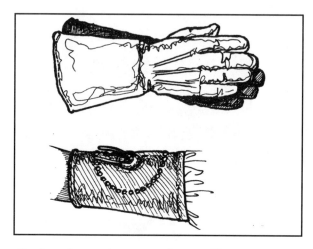

Cowboy glove and arm gauntlet or cuff.

■ Who invented the cowboy hat?

John B. Stetson invented the cowboy hat as we know it today. The story of how he developed it includes both historical fact and fiction. At the heart of the legend is an amazing American success story.

Before the mid-1800s, cowboys usually wore Mexican *sombreros* made of leather or cheap felt. After the Civil War, they started to wear the military slouch hat. Both of these hats, with their floppy brims, shaded the cowboy from the sun and protected him from rain. In fact, the word *sombrero* comes from the word *sombra*, which means "shade" in Spanish.

In the 1850s, John Stetson was working in the family business in Philadelphia. Coming from a family of hatters, he learned hat-making from his father, and he worked with his brothers making hats. Stetson developed tuberculosis and, like many others with the disease, he migrated west for his health. He eventually joined up with a party in hopes of finding gold while traveling to the Colorado territory.

Stetson "Boss of the Plains"

Old Time Floppy

Mexican Sombrero

Vaquero Poblano

Montana Peak

Modern Western

Texas Ten-Gallon

Several primary styles of cowboy hats.

Legend has it that while sitting around a campfire in 1862, Stetson decided to show his fellow travelers that a hat-making process using felt could make a large, dependable hat. From his knowledge of hat-making, Stetson knew that felt, a cloth-making process using clean beaver or rabbit fur, would make a durable fabric. He fashioned a plain felt hat resembling a modified Mexican *sombrero* using animal fur. He wore the hat and was soon approached by a fellow traveler, a horseman. The man told Stetson how much he liked the hat and offered Stetson a five-dollar gold piece for it. Stetson sold him the hat and, as they say, the rest is history.

In 1865, he returned to Philadelphia and rejoined the family business. Remembering his sale of the felt hat for five dollars, Stetson decided to make similar hats for the cowboys in the West. He soon began making hats fashioned after the felt hat he had sold to the western horseman. He shipped the hats west, and they were an immediate success.

The first hat he sold to cowboys was a hat called the "Boss of the Plains." The hat was a big, natural-colored hat with a 4-inch-tall top, a 4-inch brim, and a strap for a hatband, essentially a modified Mexican *sombrero*. Throughout the West, cowboys made the Boss of the Plains the standard cowboy hat. It was a great success and became the best-known hat west of the Mississippi River because of its high quality and durability.

The Stetson became the best-known cowboy hat ever made. Stetson hats were made of a blend of beaver, rabbit, elk, and other furs. The best hats were made of 100 percent beaver fur. When he died in 1902, Stetson was making two million hats a year.

■ How would a cowboy use his hat?

The cowboy hat was amazingly versatile, with many different uses. Its primary purpose was to shield the cowboy from the sun and protect him from the elements, especially rain. During the course of his work, the cowboy might use his hat to fan a fire, feed and water a horse, take a drink of water from a stream, wave to turn cattle in a stampede, swat a pesky insect, or roll it up as a pillow. One of the reasons the Stetson became the cowboy hat of choice was that it could be roughly used and abused and still retain its basic shape.

A cowboy using his hat to drink water from a peaceful lake.

■ Why do cowboys wear spurs?

Spurs are nicknamed "the gentle persuaders." They are used to strike the horse on its flanks to make it work harder and faster. In truth, no good cowboy uses the spurs more than sparingly, and no good cowboy ever leaves spur marks on his horse. The best cowboys prefer to guide a horse with the reins and with his good "horse sense."

The history of the spur dates back many centuries. Horsemen have used spurs since 700–500 B.C.; even Julius Caesar's legions are believed to have used them. Early spurs had single prongs and were known as prick spurs. Specimens have been found in Etruscan tombs of the second century B.C. Genghis Khan's Mongol hordes wore the prick spur in the year 1200.

It is believed that the French were the first to develop the revolving rowel spur. This type of spur came into general use by the fourteenth century. By the middle of the fifteenth century, the spur had evolved into its present design.

During this time, the spur became an indicator of one's place in the social hierarchy. Royalty and knights could wear spurs made of gold. Horsemen of lower rank would wear spurs made of silver. Even lower were spurs made of iron or tin. Legends tell of disgraced knights having their spurs cut apart in public.

Spanish *vaqueros* wore iron spurs that were similar to the large roweled spurs of the *conquistadores*—the first Spanish soldiers. Spanish armorers had developed ornate spurs with rowels up to 8 inches in diameter. Horsemen could not walk wearing these spurs. Servants had to put them on after they had mounted the horse and remove them before dismounting.

The *Grande Espuela*, the Great Spur, the Spanish *conquistador* spur.

Later Spanish spurs were more reasonably sized, but Mexican spurs characteristically still have rowels 2 to 3 inches in diameter. The working *vaquero* wore iron spurs with silver inlay decoration that had descended from the larger roweled *conquistador* spur.

The Mexican *vaquero* spur.

The Anglo settlers wore spurs that followed the English design. These were smaller than the Mexican spurs and had straighter shanks and smaller rowels.

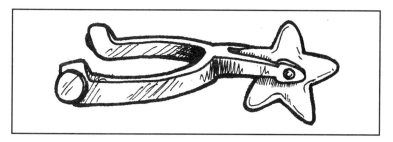

The modern work spur. The rowel on this spur is called the Texas star rowel.

Eventually, cowboys wore a large variety of spurs following both Mexican and English designs. As the look and style of spurs became more varied, a cowboy's choice of spurs became one of individual taste or preference.

■ What are the parts of a spur?

The parts of a spur are the heel band, the shank, the rowel, the chap hook, the spur strap, the spur button, the heel chains, and the jingle-bobs.

- ★ The heel band is the body of the spur and wraps around the boot heel.
- ★ The shank extends from the rear of the spur heel band and holds the rowel.
- ★ The rowel is the revolving star-shaped disk or set of pointed spikes at the end of the shank. Cowboys usually file down and blunt the rowels so they do not cut up the horse's hide.
- ★ The curved chap hook is on the top part of the shank and keeps the chaps from getting caught up in the rowel.
- ★ The spur strap holds the spur to the boot.
- ★ The spur button holds the spur strap to the spur.
- ★ The heel chains ride under the arch of the boot by the heel and keep the spur from riding up the boot.
- ★ The jingle-bobs hang from the rear of the shank and strike against the rowels as they turn, producing a sound that cowboys like a lot.

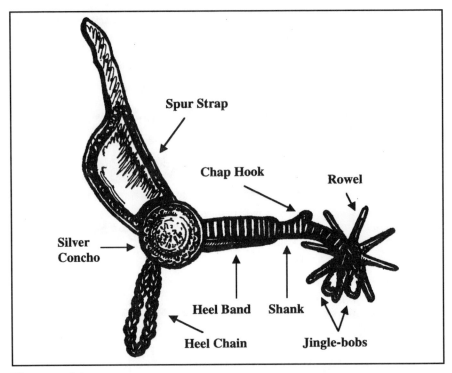

The parts of the spur.

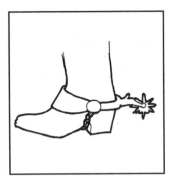

The placement of the spur on the boot.

■ Why do cowboys use a whip?

A classic western image is one of a cowboy cracking a long coiled bullwhip and the whip's sharp crack starting a herd of cattle moving up the trail drive. This image gives us the whip's most important use for a cowboy—to get the cows' attention. But, just as spurs are never used to harm a horse, a whip is never used to strike a cow.

Cowboys usually carry their whip tied to their saddle. They crack the whip over the heads of the cattle to get their attention and prepare them for moving on. Just like their roping skills, cowboys pride themselves on their skill with a whip. One old cowboy legend tells of a cowboy who could use his whip to flick a fly off the rear of a cow and not have the cow feel a thing.

Working cowboy whips are made of braided leather. They can be any length, but most working whips are between 8 and 12 feet long. At the end of the whip is a narrow strip of leather, string, or nylon. This is called the cracker or popper and is the part of the whip that makes it crack. The crack is made when the cracker changes direction with a flick of the cowboy's wrist. At this moment, the cracker is moving between 700 and 900 miles per hour and breaks the sound barrier in the same way a jet plane breaks the sound barrier and produces a sonic boom. The crack of the whip is actually the cracker breaking the sound barrier.

Cowboys also use a smaller riding whip called a *quirt*, from the Spanish phrase *cuarta de cordón*, meaning "whip of cord." The quirt is made from strips of rawhide braided together. The handle of the quirt is weighted with iron or lead shot and is usually attached to the saddle. Old-time cowboys would wrap the loop at the top of the quirt around two fingers and twirl it to strike the quirt against the horse's flanks to make the horse work harder and faster.

■ How do cowboys use ropes?

The two main skills a cowboy has to have to be successful are "ridin' and ropin'." It's hard to say which is more important because both are so necessary to managing cattle. The best cowboys, however, were masters at roping cattle.

The original *vaqueros* used long lances and hocking knives, up to 12 feet long, with crescent-shaped knives at the end, to disable the cattle by cutting their leg tendons. Once the cattle could not walk, the *vaqueros* could easily capture them. In the mid-1500s, the Spanish rancher's association, the *Mesta*, outlawed the use of the lance and the hocking knife because it disabled the cattle to an unnecessary degree. The *vaqueros* began to use rope to catch the cattle and shortly became very expert in its use.

The first ropes were braided rawhide strings. Eventually, cowboys used other materials for their ropes, including rawhide leather, fiber from the Mexican maguey plant, Manila hemp from the Philippine banana plant, horsehair, and sisal produced from the leaves of the Agave cactus. Cowboys eventually developed a preference for ropes made of Manila hemp because of how well it worked. Cowboys had a saying that a good rope would sing in the air as it was thrown. They were referring to the whistling sound a rope makes as it flies through the air.

Different materials were used according to the job at hand. Although it was strong, durable, and easily available, leather had to be treated with tallow or petrolatum and worked continuously because it had a tendency to become stiff and inflexible, especially after being wet. Rope made from the maguey plant could only be used in dry climates and was intended for light duty work. Horsehair made for a quick rope when no other materials were available, but it was not strong enough for continued use. An old cowboy legend stated that if a cowboy circled his bed site with a horsehair rope, no snake would cross its scratchy surface.

The *vaqueros* called their ropes *la reata*, which is the Spanish word for rope. Anglo cowboys changed this word into *lariat*. The English word *lasso* also came from a Spanish word—the word for snare or trap, *lazo*. Modern cowboys usually just call it "rope."

A *vaquero reata*, a *vaquero* rope.

Ropes could be from 35 to 75 feet long. Cowboy folklore tells of old-time *vaqueros* who would use ropes up to 120 feet long. Whatever the truth, long ropes were necessary to catch cattle running away from the cowboy at full speed.

Ropes had loops at the end called hondas. The hondas had leather strips in them called burners. The burners were used to keep the honda loop from wearing through under hard use.

Before the development of the prominent saddle horn for tying off rope, early *vaqueros* would tie one end of the rope to the tail of the horse and the other end to the cow. Later, cowboys developed two methods for tying the rope to the saddle horn. Cowboys became known by the method they chose to use. A cowboy was either a "dally man" or a "fast-tie man."

Dally men would loosely wrap the rope around the saddle using a slipknot. This loose wrap allowed the cowboy to quickly unwrap the rope in case the cow threatened to throw the cowboy or the horse. The word *dally* came from the Spanish phrase for the technique, *dar la vuelta*, which means "to give it a turn."

The *vaqueros* would yell to one another "*Dale, dale. Dale vuelta,* " which meant "Give it a turn." Anglo cowboys heard the "*dale*" and called the technique dally roping.

A dally loose rope tie.

Fast-tie men would tie the rope to the saddle horn with a tight, figure-eight knot. With this knot, the rope would not slip or become untied. It was a dangerous way to secure the rope to the saddle because if a cow pulled on the rope too hard, the cowboy and the horse could both be thrown down. The advantage of the fast-tie was that, if used successfully, the lassoed cow could not break loose and run away with the cowboy's rope.

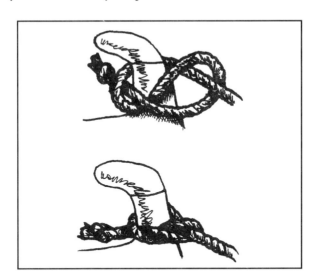

A fast figure-eight tie.

The two main types of throws were called "a header" or "a footer." The terms are self-explanatory. A "header" was a throw around the cow's head, while a "footer" was a throw around the cow's hind legs. Of course, there were many other throws depending upon the skill of the cowboy.

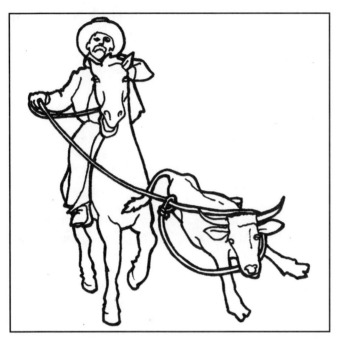

A header rope throw.

A footer rope throw.

■ How did the saddle develop?

Since the beginning of time, when men first rode horses, they rode bareback, or with only a blanket thrown over the horse's back. The development of the saddle was one of the most important advances in the history of horse riding. The saddle allows the horse rider to travel over long distances and perform work more easily. It also allowed the military soldier to fight more effectively and dominate his enemies more thoroughly.

The true origins of the saddle are lost in antiquity, but scholars have recognized that horsemen have been using the saddle since 700 B.C. The beginnings of the modern saddle originate with the Moors, who brought their saddle to Europe in the eighth century. Its design greatly influenced the eventual design of the western saddle, which is a descendant of the Moorish and Spanish war saddles.

The Moors originated the early Spanish-Moorish saddle for cavalry warfare. It was the *jineta* style, a short-stirrup saddle. The short stirrup allowed the rider to stand up in the saddle and use his lance weapons to attack other soldiers more effectively.

La brida (the Spanish war saddle) evolved after the Moorish saddle. It had longer stirrups, was heavier than the Moorish saddle, and had a tightly curved saddle seat. All of these design features held the rider in more securely.

The *silla de montar* was for the gentleman *charro* rider. It had a heavy housing, a large horn, and rich decorative ornamentation. It was used for performance riding to show off the rider's horsemanship skills.

Another ornate saddle was the *silla charra*, also a saddle for *charro* riders. It was also richly decorated with silver rosettes, silver chains and coins, and fancy leather tooling.

The regular working *vaquero* used *la silla vaquero.* It was a Mexican-designed, smaller style work saddle and is the direct ancestor of the western cowboy saddle. It had a light housing with little or no ornamentation. It was made from a light rawhide-covered wood (the wooden frame that is a saddle's base) and had a small horn and large stirrups hanging from the sides.

The western saddle that became the saddle of the working cowboy descended from the *silla vaquero.* It weighed about 40 pounds and had a high saddle horn, a raised rear cantle, and large open stirrups. The stirrups were made of bent wood and bound with iron, brass, or leather. A light Texas saddle could weigh as little as 25 pounds.

The saddle was the cowboy's most important piece of equipment. He rode in it all day and used it for a pillow at night. While the rancher supplied the horses for the trail drive, and most cowboys did not own a horse, all cowboys owned a saddle. It was their most expensive possession and usually a once-in-a-lifetime purchase. One cowboy joke said that a cowboy rode a 10-dollar horse with a 40-dollar saddle.

The saddle was so important that an expression for a man who had left cowboy work was "he's sold his saddle."

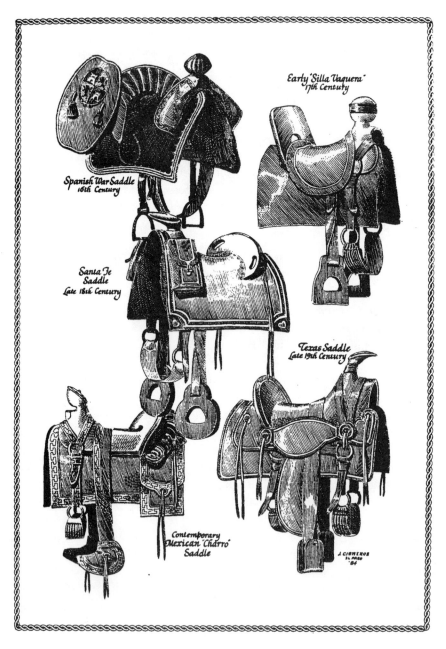

Historical versions of the saddle showing the development of the modern saddle.

■ What are the parts of a saddle?

The western saddle evolved from the Spanish saddle, specifically the *vaquero* saddle. Cowboys designed it for herding cattle. Every part of the saddle is either for the comfort of the rider and the horse or for the work duties of the cow-herding cowboy.

* ★ The first saddles had no horns. The horns were developed to help the cowboy tie off his rope. At first, the *vaqueros* tied the rope to the horse's tail. Eventually, they realized that this method was not very effective. The horn then quickly evolved to its present size and use.

* ★ The wide flaps of the saddle skirt are important because they distribute the rider's weight over a larger area of the horse's back. They also help maintain the saddle's position on the horse's back.

* ★ The saddle jockey covers the saddle skirt and adds additional stability to the saddle.

* ★ The cantle helps keep the cowboy from sliding off the rear of the saddle. It also helps create, along with the forks, a secure pocket for the rider to sit in.

* ★ The fenders keep the horse's sweat off the rider's legs.

* ★ Latigo, or saddle, strings provide useful and strong leather straps for securing items to the saddle.

* ★ The cinches secure the saddle to the horse's body.

* ★ The conchos are both decorative and useful. A decorative, fancy-tooled, metal disk, often silver, it enhances the look of the saddle. Multiple conchos add beauty to the saddle. When latigo strings are connected to them, they contribute to the securing system of the saddle.

* ★ Stirrups are the wooden or leather-covered foot holder at the sides of the saddle. A cowboy used the stirrups to secure his feet while he was in the saddle. They also helped give the rider important leverage while working in the saddle.

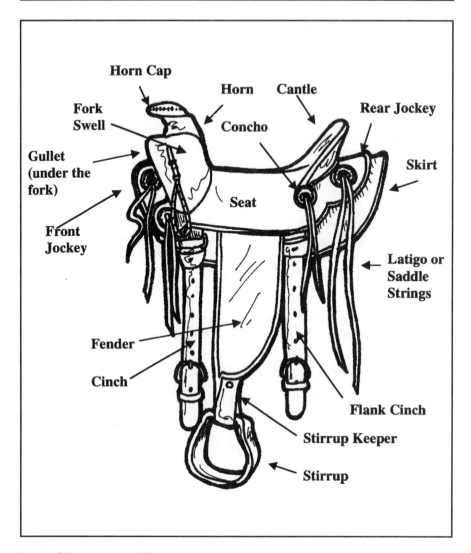

Parts of the western saddle.

The stirrups often included leather covers called *tapaderos* or taps, from the Spanish word *tapar*, meaning "to cover." These leather coverings protected the cowboy's boots. They resembled animal faces and were called eagle-, bulldog-, or monkey-face taps. Many a cowboy prided himself on controlling the horse just with gentle nudges of his taps.

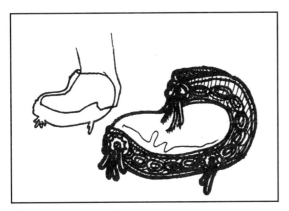

Monkey-nose *tapadero.*

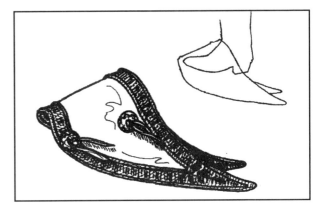

Eagle-beak *tapadero.*

■ What are chaps?

Chaps (pronounced "shaps") are seatless leather leg coverings designed to protect the cowboy's legs while riding in the rough and thorny brush or chaparral. There are three main types of chaps: shotgun chaps, bat-wing chaps, and woolies. A fourth type is called chinks.

The early *vaqueros* had large, tough leather flaps called *armas* attached to their saddles. These large *armas* developed into leg coverings when the *vaquero* detached them from the saddle and wrapped them around his legs. The Spanish called these leather leggings *chaparreras* or *chaparejos,* from *chaparro prieto,* thistle or thorn bush. The Anglo cowboys adapted these Spanish words into the word chaps.

Cowboys wearing woolies chaps.

Shotgun chaps are pants-like leather leggings that resemble the two long barrels of a shotgun. They are pulled on over regular cowboy pants. They can be difficult to wear because the cowboy has to remove his boots and spurs every time he puts them on or takes them off.

Shotgun chaps.

Bat-wing chaps are large leather flaps that wrap around the cowboy's pant legs. They are fastened together with buckles and fit loosely on the cowboy's legs. Since they can be easily unfastened, they are much easier to put on and remove than shotgun chaps.

Bat-wing chaps.

Woolies are wool-covered chaps worn during the winter. They are usually covered with Angora goat wool, but other animal fur can be used as well.

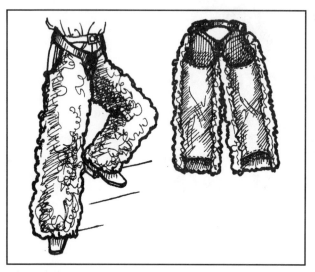

Woolies chaps.

Chinks are short, knee-length chaps. They developed from the Spanish *armitas*, a shorter and lighter version of the first *armas* leather leg coverings. Just as woolies are meant to keep the cowboy's legs warm in the winter, chinks are meant to be lighter and cooler in the summer.

Chinks chaps.

■ What kind of shirt did a cowboy wear?

A cowboy usually wore a plain, long-sleeved shirt made of cotton, wool, or flannel. A collarless shirt was the most common design. Since cowboys would not have more than one change of clothes for the whole trail drive, their shirts, like their other daily clothes, were simple and durable.

Pictures from the trail-drive era showed a variety of shirt designs on the working cowboy, but most were nothing fancy. Shirts could be solid colored or striped. Dark blue was a common color. Studio-posed pictures from the era showed fancier shirts that closely resemble the modern rodeo cowboy shirt with its collars, shield front, and mother-of-pearl buttons.

■ What kind of pants did a cowboy wear?

Cowboys wore either wool pants or cotton denim jeans. Levi Strauss first developed his cotton denim jeans for the gold miners in California, but his jeans soon became a favorite of western cowboys because of their durability.

Cowboy pants had no pockets or belt loops. A cowboy did not need anything in his pockets when he was sitting in a saddle all day.

Cowboys also wore no belt. A belt buckle would just be uncomfortable. Cowboys preferred to wear their pants tight, so a belt was unnecessary. *Vaqueros* wore a brightly colored sash around their waists.

Modern cowboys almost always wear Wrangler® brand jeans. They were designed by working cowboys and have many features especially for them. They have zippers, not buttons, wide leg bottoms to accommodate boot tops, and extra room in the seat and thigh allowing them to mount and dismount easier.

They differ from the pants of old-time cowboys in two ways. They have both pockets and belt loops. The rear pockets ride high on the jean so the cowboy does not sit on his billfold in the saddle. They also have wider belt loops and extra space between the front belt loops to accommodate the large rodeo belt buckles modern cowboys like to wear.

■ Why did cowboys wear vests?

Cowboys wore vests because their pants had no pockets. A cowboy sitting in the saddle all day did not want to be sitting on anything in his pockets. The multi-pocketed vest was the perfect piece of clothing for the cowboy. In its many deep pockets he could store tobacco, cigarette rolling paper, matches, a harmonica or mouth harp, a pencil and tally sheet for keeping track of the cows, and any other small personal items.

■ Why did cowboys use bandanas?

The bandana, also called a kerchief or "wipe," was an important part of a cowhand's gear. Usually made out of cotton, linen, or sometimes silk, it served many purposes for the working cowboy. It could be used as a towel, as a tourniquet, as a mop for wiping one's face, as a mask to filter out dust, as a tie-down for one's hat, as an earmuff in cold weather, as protection for one's hands when holding hot items such as a branding iron, as a water filter, and as an emergency sling. It could even be used to protect a cowboy's eyes from snow blindness in winter or to cover the eyes of a skittish horse while it is being saddled. The bandana really did have 1,001 uses for the cowboy.

Vaquero wearing a bandana.

■ Did cowboys really wear guns?

One of America's most potent images is of the cowboy with a six-shooter strapped to his leg, facing down a rustler with his gun or shooting up a cow town. However, the truth is very different. Cowboys generally never wore guns on a trail drive. Sitting in a saddle all day with a heavy gun and holster attached to his leg was not practical for the working cowboy.

On a trail drive, the cook kept any guns or rifles with him on the chuck wagon. Guns were used to shoot predators, to put down crippled or injured animals, to defend against Indians or rustlers, to turn aside stampedes, to kill a cow for beef to eat, or to hunt game.

■ Who invented the cowboy boot?

Historical drawings and descriptions of the first *vaqueros*, the mission Indians, have them wearing sandal-like shoes as they worked cattle. Some Indians wore their spurs attached to the rear of the sandals. This image might seem a bit far-fetched to modern cowboys, but it does reveal that the modern cowboy boot did not always exist. It was not until the 1870s that the modern cowboy boot developed its present shape.

For many generations, the cattle workers wore whatever shoes they had. For the mission Indians, it was sandals and moccasins. For farmers, it was farmer boots. For ex-soldiers, it was cavalry boots. For others, it was regular work shoes or boots.

Cowboys in the Southwest were exposed to the Spanish and Mexican *vaquero* and *charro* boots. The Spanish had a well-developed tradition of leather boot-making, with the most wealthy gentlemen riders wearing tall, fancy-tooled boots decorated with silver ornamentation. Eventually, the Anglo cowboys developed their own style of boots suited to the rough work of herding cattle.

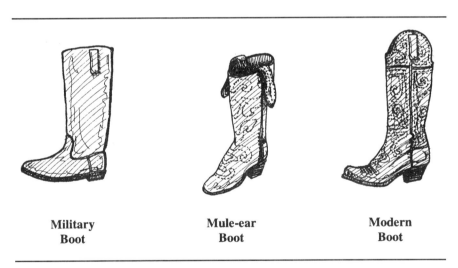

Military Boot	**Mule-ear Boot**	**Modern Boot**

Cowboy boot styles.

Early cowboy boots resembled military boots. They had a stovepipe top rising up to the knees, with a flat heel and a round toe. Some boots had what was called a coffin toe because it was squared off like the end of a coffin box. Large mule-ear bootstraps helped the cowboy pull the boots on.

An early cowboy boot was the Coffeyville boot. A bootmaker by the name of J. W. Cubine in Coffeyville, Kansas, made what became known as Coffeyville

Boots. They were patterned after the English Wellington and U.S. cavalry boots with a tall top that was straight across the back and rounded in front, reaching up to just above the knee. It had a high heel and a broad, rounded toe.

As with many other cowboy events, a legend exists in cowboy folklore about the invention of the modern-style boot. The story says that Charles Hyer of Olathe, Kansas, on the western outskirts of Kansas City, was the first bootmaker to construct the modern boot.

According to the legend, a cowboy getting off a cattle drive in Kansas City in 1875 or 1876 did what most cowboys did at the end of a cattle drive: he threw away his old boots and went to buy a new pair of handmade boots. He went to Hyer's boot shop and asked Hyer to make him a boot that did not look like the usual military boot. He described a boot with a pointed toe, a slanted heel, and a high top that was scalloped in the front and back rather than the stovepipe style. Hyer made the boots for the cowboy, who happily walked away in them. Other cowboys saw the new boots, liked them, and went to Hyer to get a pair made for themselves. Soon Hyer's boot became the preferred style of cowboy boot.

Of course, the legend has its supporters and detractors. Others state that H. J. Justin developed the first modern-style boot. According to this version of boot history, Justin moved from Indiana in 1879 and settled in Spanish Fort, Texas. He began a business as a boot repairman and was soon making cowboy boots for cowboys driving cattle up the Chisholm Trail. Justin's boots eventually became known as "The Standard of the West."

Just as the Stetson hat became the preferred brand of cowboy hat, Hyer and Justin boots became the cowboy's boot of choice. By the 1880s, the modern design was prevalent throughout the West. Cowboys recognized that its design made it ideally suited for cattle and horse work, and its design has changed little in the following years.

■ How much did cowboy boots cost?

Cowboys coming off the trail usually threw away their old boots and had new custom boots made for them. Cowboys were vain about their feet and liked them to look as small as possible. They had their boots made as small as possible to still fit on their feet.

The boots cost from $10 to $15 a pair. While this seems cheap by modern standards, cowboys only made about $25 to $40 a month while on the trail drive.

■ Why does the cowboy boot look like it does?

The cowboy boot has three distinctive features: a tall leather upper, a pointed toe, and a raked or sloped heel. Each of these features evolved specifically to protect the cowboy and to help make his work easier.

The tall leather upper protects the cowboy's ankles and lower legs from the thorny brush. The pointed toe makes it easier for the boot to find and slide into the stirrup. The raked heel helps the cowboy's foot stay hooked to the stirrup.

A raked heel is important because most injuries are horse related, and the greatest fear a cowboy has is of being "hung up." When a cowboy is "hung up," he has been thrown from his horse, and his foot is stuck in the stirrup as the horse drags him. The raked heel helps the cowboy secure his foot in the stirrup during a rough ride.

Because of its high raked heel, cowboy boots can be awkward to walk in. Cowboys did not worry about this because a real cowboy never walked when he did not have to. In fact, cowboys literally and figuratively looked down on a man who was "afoot." Also, being thrown from one's horse and left "afoot" was a great danger for a cowboy as well as an embarrassment. A cowboy who was "afoot" was stranded far from the ranch or range camp without a horse to transport him. He was alone and vulnerable to the dangers of the open range.

■ What did cowboys sleep on?

During the trail drive, a cowboy usually slept out on the open range or in small pup tents. Either way the cowboy would sleep in a large bedroll. The bedroll was made of heavy, large canvas, as large as 7 feet by 17 feet. The canvas tarp bedroll also included a blanket or a quilt, which was also called a soogan.

The bedroll was the cowboy's suitcase. In it he kept items such as spare clothes, equipment, and his "warbag" (a small bag in which he kept his personal belongings).

Because they were too large to carry on a horse, the bedrolls were carried on the chuck wagon or in a separate bedroll wagon.

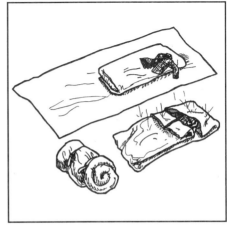

Cowboy bedroll. A cowboy wraps up for protection from the rain.

Cowboys sleeping in their bedrolls outside the bunkhouses on a hot night. This photograph is of cowboys at the W. D. Boyce Cattle Company in Kansas.

Chuck wagon with bedrolls piled on top.

3

The Great Trail Drives

The Glory Days of the Cowboy

■ Why did cattlemen start the trail drives?

The main reason cattlemen started the trail drives was because a great profit could be made in driving cattle from south Texas to the railheads in Kansas. A cow worth 5 dollars in Texas could bring 40 dollars when sold in Kansas. As soon as cattlemen realized that driving cattle north could make a lot of money, the great trail drives began.

From the early days of the Spanish colonial era, cattle had roamed freely on the open ranges, and their numbers increased greatly. By 1775, south Texas was teeming with wild cattle, and by the early 1800s some estimates held that millions of cattle were in Texas. There were so many cattle that they had almost no value at all; there were no markets for them, there were too many of them, and nobody owned them anyway.

During the Spanish period of Texas history, the market for Texas long-horns was very limited. Even into the 1840s and 1850s, the only use for Texas cattle was for hides for leather goods and tallow for soap and candles.

The trail-drive era got off to a slow start. In the 1700s, early cattle drives went east to Louisiana where there was a market for cattle by-products. *Vaqueros* also drove some of these cattle to Coahuila, Mexico. Later, during the Civil War, Texas was a major supplier of beef for the Confederacy. Even with these markets, the demand for Texas cattle remained small.

When gold was discovered in California in 1848, the gold rush instantly created a new market. To take advantage of this new cattle market, a few cattlemen started cattle drives traveling along the Old Spanish Trail from San Antonio to California. These cattlemen established several trails from Texas to California and demonstrated that cattle could be driven long distances to market. By the late 1850s, however, the California market for Texas beef ended as California developed its own beef supplies.

The 1800s saw a steep rise in European immigration on the East Coast. These growing multitudes created a need for beef. With millions of head of cattle in Texas, with slaughterhouses in Chicago and St. Louis, and with a growing demand for beef in the large East Coast cities, it was just a matter of time before Texas cattlemen realized the huge profits waiting for them if they could figure out a way to get the cattle to the slaughterhouses. At the end of the Civil War, the stage was set for the beginning of the great trail drives.

■ Who started the trail drives?

Joseph McCoy is generally credited with being the "father of the cow town." McCoy was one of the first to realize that a great profit was possible if the millions of cattle in south Texas could be taken to the Chicago slaughterhouses. In the 1860s, he persuaded the Kansas Pacific Railroad to set special rates for shipping cattle from Kansas to Chicago, a major meat-packing center. McCoy selected Abilene, Kansas, for his first railhead because the land was cheap and available.

In 1867, McCoy established Abilene as a railhead depot. McCoy sent word to Texas that he was ready to ship cattle to Chicago from Abilene. In five years, 1.5 million head arrived in Abilene from Texas.

■ Where did the trail drives go?

As soon as Joseph McCoy had established Abilene as a cow town, cattlemen in south Texas began driving their cattle north. Over the 20-year history of the trail drive, four great trails developed: the Shawnee Trail, the Chisholm Trail, the Western Trail, and the Goodnight-Loving Trail.

The Shawnee Trail was the first trail to take cattle north. It was first used from 1846 to 1861. After the end of the Civil War, it ran for two short years from 1865 to 1866. The trail began in south Texas and traveled north to Dallas. It then curved northeast along the Red River to the northern border of Texas. It passed through Indian Territory into the northeastern corner of Kansas, traveled on to Kansas City, to Sedalia, and finally to St. Louis, another beef-packing center. The Shawnee Trail never developed into an important high-traffic trail like the others did.

The Chisholm Trail was the first famous trail drive. It existed from 1867 to 1884. It was the trail that ended at the first great cow town, Abilene, Kansas. It was named for Jessie Chisholm, a half-white, half-Cherokee trader who had established several trading posts in the Indian Territory, in what is now Oklahoma. The trails he had developed between his trading posts were clear paths for the early trail drives. The Chisholm Trail originated in south Texas, traveled north through the Dallas–Ft. Worth area, and then up to Abilene.

The Western Trail was a branch of the Chisholm Trail. It ran from 1867 to the 1890s. After following the Chisholm Trail across Indian Territory, cowboys angled northwest to the last of the great cow towns, Dodge City.

Charles Goodnight and Oliver Loving had a different idea about where markets for Texas cattle might be. They knew of the gold mines in the Rocky Mountains and felt that a market for Texas beef could be developed in the mountain mining camps. The Goodnight-Loving Trail ran from 1866 to 1875. It originated in south-central Texas and traveled west through central Texas into southern New Mexico. Once in New Mexico, cowboys turned north and continued on to Colorado, Wyoming, and Montana.

■ What were some of the famous cattle towns?

The first of the famous cow towns, which were destination towns for the cattle drives, was Abilene, Kansas. Joseph McCoy established Abilene as a cow town in 1867 when he built a railhead depot for shipping cattle to Chicago.

McCoy had been searching for a site for the first railhead because the Kansas legislature had established a quarantine line and was not allowing Texas cattle into Kansas because of the tick fever carried by Texas longhorns. The longhorns were immune to the tick fever poison, but they were carriers, and the fever killed Kansas cattle. Since Abilene was west of the quarantine line, Texas cattle could travel across Kansas to it; and because the land was cheap, McCoy selected Abilene.

In a pattern that was to be repeated in all the cow towns, the citizens of Abilene drove the cattle business out of town after five years. The citizens had tired of

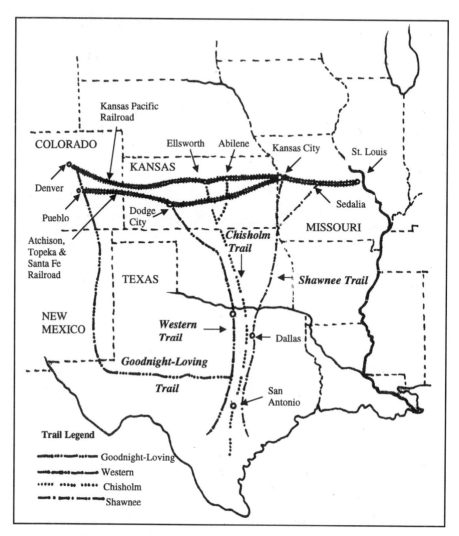

The routes of the great trail drives.

the rowdy activities the cowboys brought to the town at the end of a month-long trail drive.

The cattle business moved west to Ellsworth in 1872. Beginning in 1872, cowboys also drove cattle to another railhead in Wichita, 85 miles south of Abilene. Other Kansas cow towns were Hayes City, Ellsworth, and Newton. The cattle business finally moved west to Dodge City, the last of the cow towns. Dodge City lasted for ten years, the longest run of any of the cow towns.

In 1884, the Kansas legislature quarantined the whole state. The anti-cattle forces in Kansas had succeeded in shutting down Kansas as a cow-town state.

■ What time of year did the trail drives take place?

The trail drives usually took place twice a year. In the spring, the cattle were rounded up, herded together, sorted, and branded. Some cattle drives took place right after the spring roundup so as to get underway when the spring grasses were up, before the rivers were swollen, and before the blistering heat of the summer would make the cattle drives even more difficult.

Other cattlemen would send their cattle to summer pastures to allow them to grow and put on more weight. Since cattlemen were paid according to the weight of the cattle when delivered at the railhead, fatter cows meant more profit.

A second roundup took place in the early fall where, once again, the cattle were herded, sorted, and branded. The cattle were then driven to market before the winter snowfalls set in, causing another type of difficulty for the trail drives.

■ How long did trail drives last?

A trail drive usually lasted three to four months.

■ How many miles did the trail drive cover each day?

On days when nothing unusual happened, the trail drive could cover 10 to 15 miles per day.

■ What was the daily routine on a trail drive?

On the first few days of the trail drive, the cowboys drove the cows a little harder and faster than they would later in the trail drive to "trail break" the herd as quickly as possible. At the beginning of a trail drive, the cattle would keep trying to return to their familiar grazing lands. They also would try to return to the last place where they drank water. To make the cattle forget their usual grazing and watering lands, the cowboys quickened the pace for the first few days.

The cattle soon settled into their routine. A lead cow quickly established itself. This cow had an aggressive temperament and stayed at the head of the herd, followed by other lead cows, for the entire drive.

Trail drive with lead cow at the head of the herd. The cowboys are at their assigned places, and one cowboy chases a stray. circa 1882–1890.

The most famous lead cow was on one of the Goodnight-Loving trail drives. The cow was named "Old Blue." Old Blue was such a good lead cow that Charles Goodnight decided not to sell it at market. He had the cowboys bring Old Blue back with them and, with a bell dangling around his neck, Old Blue led cattle on trail drives for seven more years.

Sick, infirm, and young cattle walked at the rear of the trail drive. Every day cattle settled into the same positions on the trail drive and retained these positions for the entire time. The cattle walked in an elongated wedge, each in its self-determined and never-varying position.

After the trail drive was under way, a regular routine was established. Before dawn, the cook woke the cowboys and fed them breakfast. The cowboys then drove the cattle five to seven miles before noon. At noontime, they found a good pasture to stop and let the cattle rest and feed. Resting and feeding the cattle along the trail was very important because the cowboys needed to bring the cattle to market weighing as much as possible. If the pace was too quick and the cattle did not have enough opportunities for feeding, they would lose weight and be less valuable at the end of the trail.

Cowboys gathered around the chuck wagon for a meal.

After the noon break, the cowboys would drive the cattle another five to seven miles before bedding them down for the night. After finding a good spot for bedding the cattle down, the cowboys would "ride 'em down": steer the cattle into walking in a circle. When the front of the herd (the point) met up with the rear of the herd (the drag) the cattle would mill around eating until they settled down for a night's sleep.

The cowboys would ride herd two at a time, in opposite directions, throughout the night. They would circle the herd, singing, making sure it stayed settled and did not stampede. The cowboys rode herd in two-hour shifts with every cowboy, except the cook, taking a turn.

The last thing the cook did every night was point the wagon tongue to the North Star so the cowboys would know which direction they were heading when the drive resumed the next morning. In the morning the cook would wake the cowboys, and the whole process would begin again. The cowboys never took a day off. They rode straight through for three to four months until the herd reached the railhead.

■ Who were the cowboys on the trail drives?

Generally, the men on the trail drive were young men. The work was hard and challenging, and strong, healthy young men were best suited for the task. They were usually in their late teens and early 20s. The trail boss might be an older, more experienced cowboy. The cook was usually an older cowboy who had left the regular hard work of the trail and had "retired" to trail-drive cooking.

Cowboys on the trail drive.

A wide range of men rode the trail drive. Ex-Civil War soldiers, ex-slaves, free men, and farm boys all rode the trail. There were Mexican *vaqueros*, Scottish, Irish, and German men. In short, cowboy trail drivers were as varied a mix of men as populated the American West at that time.

One of the most interesting types of trail drivers was the "remittance man." This man was usually a well-educated British gentleman who had come to the American West to start a new life. For one reason or another, he had been unsuccessful in his former life and his family had sent him to America. He received regular payments of money (remittances) from his family; thus, the name.

■ How many cowboys were on a trail drive?

A trail drive usually had between eight to twelve cowboys, plus a trail boss and a cook. Each cowboy was responsible for 200 to 300 cattle.

In all, between 30,000 and 40,000 cowboys rode the trail drives during their 20-year history.

■ What were the jobs on the trail drives?

The trail boss was the leader of the trail drive. He was usually an older, more experienced cowboy. The trail boss rode at the head of the herd and scouted ahead for places to feed and bed the cattle. He also selected the best place to cross a river. The eight to twelve cowboys who rode the trail drive worked for the trail boss.

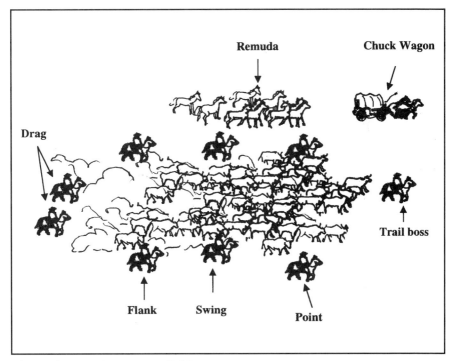

The cowboy positions on a trail drive.

Behind the trail boss were the point men, also more experienced cowboys, who rode directly at the front of the herd, leading it down the trail.

The next two jobs on the trail drive were riding swing and riding flank. These two positions rode at the sides of the herd and were responsible for keeping it intact and making sure no cattle strayed away.

The drag riders had the unpleasant job of riding at the rear of the herd. This was the worst job on the trail drive because the cowboys riding drag had to work hard to keep the sick, infirm, and younger cattle from falling behind. Cows that were too lazy to keep up with the herd were also a problem for the drag riders. Making the job even more difficult, the drag riders rode all day in the dust of the

2,000 to 3,000 cattle. The drag riders were usually the youngest, least experienced cowboys on the trail drive.

The *remudero*, or horse wrangler, was another job on the trail drive. The *remuda* was the herd of horses that the cowboys rode. Each cowboy had about six to eight horses he rode during the trail drive. A *remuda* could have as many as 100 horses. The cowboys would change horses every few hours so they were always riding a fresh one. The *remudero* was the cowboy who took care of the horses on a trail drive. He gathered the horses throughout the day to be available for the cowboys, and at night he constructed a makeshift corral with rope and watched the horses throughout the night. The *remudero* was usually the first job a young cowboy had on a trail drive. The *remudero* was considered the lowest level job on a trail drive; the bottom layer of the cowboy hierarchy.

The horse *remuda*, a rope corral on a trail drive.

Rivaling the trail boss as the most important job on a trail drive was the cook. The cook was usually an older cowboy who had retired from the hard work of driving the cows. All the cowboys tried to stay on the cook's good side and the success or failure of many a trail drive was determined by how good the cook was.

■ How much were cowboys paid on the trail drive?

Cowboys were hired laborers working for cattle owners to drive the cattle to the railheads. The cattle owners made large profits on the trail drives, but the cowboys working the trail drives made very little money.

* The trail boss was the highest-paid cowboy on a trail drive. He earned about $150 a month.

* The cook was the second-highest-paid person on the trail drive. He usually made about $50 to $75 a month.

* The regular cowboys were the lowest-paid workers on a trail drive. They usually made between $25 to $40 a month.

At the end of a trail drive, after buying new clothes and boots, buying a nice meal, taking a bath, and celebrating the end of the trail drive, a cowboy would have very little money left. Often cowboys ended the trail drive as poor as when they started.

■ What type of jobs did horses have on a trail drive?

The romantic cowboy image always includes the cowboy and his horse, inseparable and dependent upon each other for survival and companionship. Indeed, many of the movie cowboys had horses as famous as they were. Roy Rogers had Trigger, and the Lone Ranger had Silver. But, the truth about the real cowboy on the trail drive was very different.

To begin with, cowboys did not own the horses they rode. They owned only their saddles, and the cattleman organizing the trail drive supplied their horses.

No cowboy rode just one horse. Each trail drive had six to eight horses for each cowboy. Cowboys would change horses several times a day, riding each horse for only three or four hours at a time. They changed horses frequently in order to rest the horses and always have a fresh ride.

Different horses were also chosen according to the job the cowboy needed to do. Each horse was a kind of specialist, excelling in one specific activity over others.

* The cutting horse was the best-trained horse, usually a fast and agile quarter horse. The cutting horse specialized in quick, sharp turns, a necessary skill when separating calves and cattle out of the herd.

* The roping horse was a good all-around horse, able to chase a running cow and stop dead on the spot when a cow had been roped.

* A river horse could swim easily in deep water. A good river horse was very helpful, because taking cattle across a river was one of the most difficult and dangerous jobs on a trail drive.

* The trail horse was a strong, dependable horse best suited for the long daily job of walking alongside the traveling herd.

* The night horse was an older horse, not easily spooked, and was a steady ride at night when "riding herd," circling and watching the sleeping herd at night.

■ How did cowboys break and train horses for the trail drive?

At the time of the trail drives, large herds of horses—wild mustangs—ran free on the open ranges. In order to have all the horses necessary for a trail drive, the cowboys had to capture, break, and train wild horses. Every ranch or cowboy outfit had a specialist who could break a horse's wild spirit and make it available for training as a trail-drive horse.

The *vaqueros* had the *amansador,* or tamer, who could break wild horses. After the *vaqueros,* the man who broke horses was called a "bronc buster."

After the cowboy had captured a wild mustang, the bronc buster took over. Every bronc buster had many methods for breaking a horse. Every horse had a different personality, and each required a different method if the breaking was to be successful. Usually, horses were about four years old when they were selected for breaking.

The first step was to put the horse in a corral and get it accustomed to a raw-hide noseband and a light leather bridle. The noseband was called a "bosal," and the bridle a "hackamore." The bronc buster tried to get the horse to react to pressure on the nose and then to pressure on the reins.

The next step was to put a bit—a metal bar—into the horse's mouth. The final step was to put a saddle on the horse and get it to accept a rider on its back.

The steps described above represent the perfect process, which hardly ever happened. Usually, horses fought every step of the breaking and resisted every new piece of equipment. The image of a wildly bucking horse trying to throw off the saddle or the rider was what usually happened when breaking horses.

Frederic Remington illustration of two cowboys breaking a horse.

Bronc busters often had to "rough break" a horse. This involved any number of rough techniques to break the horse's wild spirit. Cowboys would twist the horse's ear so the pain would distract the horse while the saddle was put on or the rider mounted it. They would rope their legs together, blindfold them, or hit them with a quirt. Sometimes they would "sack out," put a sack of grain on the horse so it would get used to carrying weight on its back. They would swing a yellow rain slicker at the horse's head so it would get used to distractions.

A cowboy would use any strategy if it would help break the horse. Some horses broke quickly and easily, and some were broken enough to be trained, but they would always be a rough ride. Some were never broken at all. Cowboys just let these horses loose again, because they would never be a dependable work horse anyway.

Generally, even though it was a tough experience for both the horse and the bronc buster, the horse would be broken and ready for training. The cowboys would then learn the natural temperaments and abilities of each horse and train them for the various jobs on the trail drive.

■ How did cowboys gather cattle for the trail drives?

Cowboys began the year by gathering cattle in the spring for the roundup. After a winter of grazing, the cows were ready to be gathered, sorted, and branded.

The *vaqueros* called this cattle hunt or gathering the *rodeo*, a Spanish word meaning to "gather" or "round up." The word eventually evolved into the word for the cowboy skill contests called rodeos.

Cowboys from several ranches would join in searching the open ranges for cattle and herding them to a common roundup location. Because all the cattle were mixed together, the cowboys had to look at the brands on the older cows to begin to sort them into groups according to which owner's brand was on each cow. Newly born calves stay close to their mothers, so the cowboys were able to place the new calves with the correct group.

The cowboys then used cutting horses to cut the new, unbranded calves away from their mothers. Then they roped the calves and dragged them to the branding station. After they branded the calves with the owner's brand, the cowboys released them to return to their mothers and the rest of the herd.

After the branding was completed, the cowboys drove the cattle to the summer range. Sometimes cowboys would begin the trail drive after the spring roundup before the heat of the summer was too severe.

At the close of summer, when the cattle were beefed up from a summer of grazing, the cowboys would gather the cattle together again. They would then select the cattle to be sold at market and form the herd for the trail drive. The trail drive would begin before the fall and winter snow and cold set in.

■ How many cattle were on a trail drive?

A typical trail drive would have 2,000 to 3,000 cattle on it. Of course, some trail drives had less, and some had more. The largest trail drive on record had more than 15,000 cattle.

■ Why did the cowboys brand cows?

For more than 4,000 years, people have branded cattle for identification purposes. The ancient Romans, Greeks, and Egyptians all branded their cattle.

The Spanish brought the practice to the New World. The Spanish *conquistador* Hernán Cortés branded his cattle with three Christian crosses on the cow's sides between the ribs and hip. The crosses represented the Father, Son, and Holy Ghost.

In 1537, the Spanish established the New World's first cattleman's association, the *Mesta*. The *Mesta* was responsible for organizing the growing Spanish cattle industry. It quickly decreed that all cattle had to be branded for ownership identification.

Since cattle roamed freely over the large ranges of New Spain, it was difficult to keep track of them. The owners of the herds needed a system of positive ownership identification. Cattle were valuable resources and correct ownership identification was very important. To protect the wealth they had in their herds, cattle owners branded all their cattle so there would be no doubt as to ownership.

In 1776, the Spanish government proclaimed that all unbranded cattle would become government property. This proclamation stimulated Spanish cattle owners to make sure all their cattle were branded.

The Spanish owners branded their cattle with *fierros*, the Spanish word for "irons." They heated these irons until they were red-hot and could burn a brand into the side of the cattle. The Spanish brands were very distinctive and had elaborate shapes and designs with curlicues and pendants.

One example was José Antonio Navarro's brand. In 1838, he registered his brand, which incorporated the initials of his name. Other examples of Spanish brands show the fancy, curved-line brand designs the Spanish used.

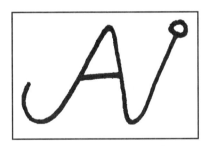

José Antonio Navarro's brand.

By the time the Texas cattlemen started the trail drives, the Spanish practice of branding cattle was firmly established. The Texas cattlemen were unable, however, to read the elaborate designs of the Spanish and Mexican brands. They called them *quien sabes*, which means "who knows?" in English.

The Texas cattlemen quickly adopted the Spanish and Mexican practice of branding cattle but developed their own brands, consisting of straight lines and well-defined letters, numbers, and symbols. The spring roundups were organized to gather and brand the newborn calves so that the herd was positively identified.

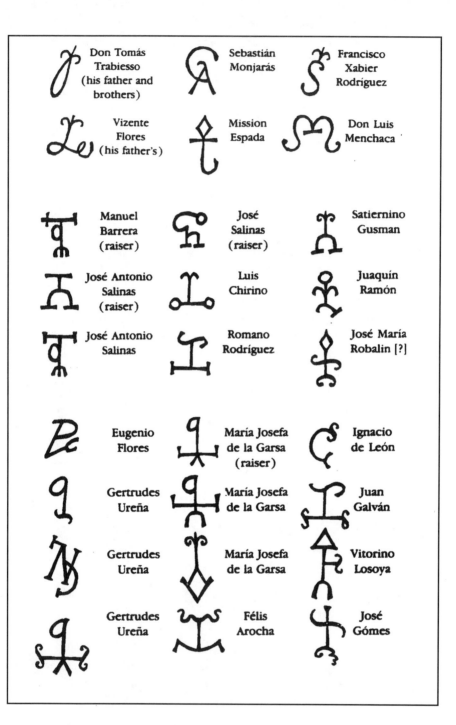

Examples of Spanish brands.

In Texas, cattle branding was especially important because of cattle theft. Cattle rustlers would capture unbranded cattle and claim them for their own. They would also steal cattle and change brands using a running iron, a curved piece of branding iron about six inches long. In some parts of the West, just possessing a running iron was enough to get a person hanged for being a cattle rustler.

Well-defined brands were also important for settling arguments over cattle ownership on the open range. Cowboys would gather cattle during the spring roundups, and they would sort the cattle according to their brands. Even with the practice of branding widely accepted and well known, cowboys still had confrontations over cattle ownership. Clear brands were one way to avoid these confrontations.

Cattle would first wear the owner's brand. Because owners would often sell cattle to each other, it was necessary to add a separate trail brand to a herd so the cowboys could accurately identify all the cattle on their own trail drive.

Frederic Remington illustration of cowboys arguing over a brand.

■ How did the cowboys brand cattle?

Branding cattle was a highly valued cowboy skill. Not every cowboy was adept at branding because it requires a careful touch. First, the iron must be at just the right temperature. An iron that's too hot will burn a cow's flesh too deeply. It might also leave an open wound that can become infected. An iron that's too cold will form a "cold brand," which leaves a sore spot on the cow, but no permanent brand.

Cowboys branding a calf.

The cowboys would heat the branding irons over an open fire. Dozens of irons would be in the fire, one for each cattle owner participating in the roundup. Cowboys would hold down the cow, select the correct branding iron, and then apply the iron to the cow's side. They would then release the calf or cow to return to the herd.

Branding irons heating over an open fire.

Cowboys could apply the brand anywhere on the cow. Eventually, custom determined that the left hip was the best place for a brand. If a cow had more than one brand, the brands could fill the whole side of a cow.

Cowboys used two types of branding irons. One was a stamping iron, about three feet long, with a handle at one end that the cowboy used to control the iron while branding. The die, or stamp end, of the iron held the brand's design. The end of the iron had a blunt, flat edge. Cowboys used the stamping iron to press and burn a brand into a cow's hide.

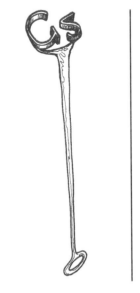

A stamping branding iron.

The second type of branding iron was the running iron. The running iron could be curled or angled at the branding end. Cowboys used the running iron as a hot pencil with which they drew a brand into the cow's hide. Brands applied with a running iron had a loose, more fluid look.

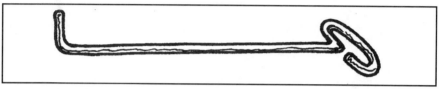

A running branding iron.

The running iron made it very easy for cowboys to change brands. As previously mentioned, in some areas of the West, mere possession of a running iron was proof of cattle rustling and could result in a frontier-justice type of hanging.

■ How big were brands?

Brands were as big as they had to be for the cowboy to be able to read them easily from horseback. Some cattlemen went overboard and had brands as large as the side of the cow. Usually, however, they were from three to six inches in size. Horses had smaller brands than cattle.

■ How did cowboys read brands?

Cowboys could read and identify hundreds of brands. One of the necessary skills for a cowboy was the ability to recognize and identify any brand he saw on a cow during the roundup and on the trail drive.

Cowboys read brands according to a well-defined and universally recognized visual system. They read brands from left to right, top to bottom, and outside to inside.

A brand leaning to one side was called a tumbling brand. An upside-down brand was called a crazy brand. A brand lying on its side was called a lazy brand. A brand stretched out with no sharp angles was called a running brand. A brand with sharp extensions or flanges at the bottom was called a walking brand. Two letters attached together made a connected brand. A brand with short strokes or wings at the top was a flying brand. A brand sitting atop a curved circle was a rocking brand.

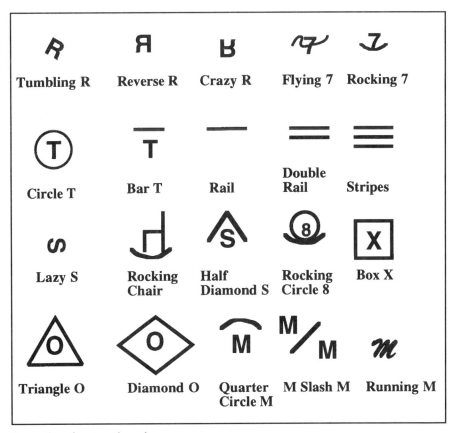

Examples of various brands.

■ Who invented the chuck wagon?

The chuck wagon was one of the great inventions that contributed to the success of the trail drives. The word *chuck* was cowboy slang for food, and it correctly identified the chuck wagon as the trail drive's food wagon.

Cattle baron Charles Goodnight was the first man to develop the chuck wagon. He recognized a need to feed the cowboys on the trail drives. Before the chuck wagon, cowboys would each carry their own food with them. The chuck wagon allowed trail drives to cover longer distances and last longer by bringing along a larger and more dependable food supply.

In 1866, Goodnight took a surplus army wagon—some say a Civil War military ambulance—and converted it to a chuck wagon. He chose the army wagon because of its large, strong, iron axles. Eventually, commercial builders sold chuck wagons for $75 to $100.

The standard features of the chuck wagon were a large wagon bed for carrying supplies, a canvas top for protecting the wagon bed and its contents, a water barrel, a honeycombed chuck box at the rear containing many small storage boxes, and a hinged table at the rear.

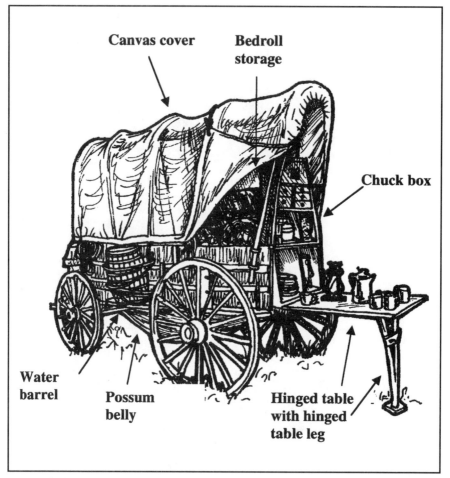

Canvas cover

Bedroll storage

Chuck box

Water barrel

Possum belly

Hinged table with hinged table leg

A typical chuck wagon.

The chuck box and the hinged table at the rear were the important innovations of the chuck wagon. The box allowed the cook to carry his ingredients and food items for cooking, and the table provided a surface for preparing food.

The chuck wagon also had a toolbox. Cowboys carried such items as guns, ammunition, tools, wheel grease, tobacco, branding irons, razors, cutting tools, horseshoeing equipment, and medical supplies in the toolbox.

Cowboys also carried a rudimentary supply of medicine on the trail drive. They carried castor oil, calomel (a white powder used as both a fungicide and a laxative), liniment for sore muscles, quinine for fever, and whiskey. Even though cowboys were not allowed to drink on a trail drive, the chuck wagon carried whiskey for medicinal purposes.

A wooden box under the rear of the wagon carried the heavy cast-iron Dutch ovens and skillets. The Dutch ovens were large pots used for cooking over the open fire.

Cowboys attached a large canvas or cow's hide under the chuck wagon. The canvas, called the "possum's belly," was used to hold the wood chips or cow or buffalo chips for the cooking fires. Cowboys called the dried cow or buffalo chips "prairie coal."

■ Who was the cook on a trail drive?

The cook on a trail drive was usually an older, retired cowboy. The cowboys nicknamed the cook "cookie" or "the old lady." The cook was second in pay to the trail boss, making about $50 to $75 per month on the trail drive.

The success of the trail drive depended on the cook. The quality of food on the trail drive could make or break morale, and the cowboys went out of their way to stay on the cook's good side.

The cook was also responsible for many other duties on the drive. He cut hair, shaved beards, dispensed medicine, and doctored wounds. The cook was the hardest- and longest-working cowboy on the trail drive. He cooked three meals a day, and he tended to all the cowboys' needs. He was the first one up in the morning and the last one to bed at night. His last duty at the end of the day was to point the wagon's tongue to the North Star so the trail boss would know which way to start the herd in the morning.

■ What did cowboys eat on the trail drive?

A cowboy's diet on a trail drive was very plain. Because all the food had to be carried on the chuck wagon, and it all had to be cooked over an open fire, there was very little variety.

The cook used staples such as flour, beans, salt pork, and rice to make most of the cowboys' meals, using sugar and spices to flavor the food. He'd keep a sourdough batch always available for making sourdough biscuits. He also carried a small amount of canned fruit. Sometimes the cowboys would trade a cow from the herd to a farmer for some eggs and fresh vegetables. As a rare and special treat, sometimes the cook would bake a fruit pie for the cowboys. Another special treat for the cowboys was hoecakes, small cakes of cornmeal eaten with molasses. Cowboys nicknamed molasses syrup "lick."

Another cook's specialty was S-O-B stew. Cowboys would say the cook threw everything from a cow into the stew except the hair and the horns. In truth, S-O-B stew was a concoction of everything the cook had to put into it.

Of course, strong coffee was an important staple of the cowboy world. Cowboys joked that they liked their coffee strong enough to float a horseshoe or melt a spoon. Arbuckle brand coffee was a cowboy favorite because of the piece of peppermint rock candy that was in every can of coffee. The cook would usually offer the candy to the cowboy who would help the cook in his work.

Wyoming cowboys going to dinner.

■ Did the cowboys ever kill a cow and eat it on the trail drive?

Cowboys would sometimes slaughter a cow to have meat on the trail drive. It would seem that with so many cattle available on a trail drive, cowboys would have a steady supply of meat. There were two problems though that kept the cowboys from always slaughtering cows to eat on the trail drive. First, the cows were more valuable when they were sold at the railhead. If they killed a lot of cows to eat during the drive, the cattle owner made less money at the end. Second, there was no way to preserve the meat, and it quickly spoiled in the hot weather.

When the cowboys did butcher a cow, they killed it late in the evening so it would stay cool in the night air. They cut the meat into strips and dried it over the campfire. Any leftover meat went into the cook's S-O-B stew.

■ What did the cook use to cook on the trail drive?

The cook used heavy cast-iron pots called Dutch ovens to cook the meals. They also used iron skillets. Because the stove was a hole in the ground, and because all the cooking was done over open fires, pots and pans had to be very durable.

The cook used porcelain-covered tin coffee pots, plates, and cups to serve the food. Because life on a trail drive was very rough, metal dishes and containers were used.

■ How did cowboys wash their dishes and clothes?

Cowboys washed everything in the "wreck pan," a metal tub carried in the chuck wagon.

Cowboy washing clothes in a "wreck pan."

■ Did cowboys really sing around the campfire at night?

The romantic movie image of cowboys sitting around the campfire singing and enjoying an evening of easy friendship is not really true. Most of the time, the cowboys were too tired from a day's work and knew they would be up for most of the night taking their turn riding herd and watching the cattle. Their usual routine was to eat, rest, and ride their two-hour night shifts.

However, the cowboys did sing to the cattle to keep them calm during the night. For some reason the singing helped keep the cattle calm and helped avoid the dreaded stampede. Cowboys would sing all the songs they knew and often improvised songs on the spot as they rode endlessly around the herd. The cows did not seem to care whether the cowboy had a good singing voice or not.

If they had time, cowboys did enjoy playing cards and talking. If they told stories, they were stories of adventures and tall tales.

Instruments were rare on a trail drive. They were too fragile and could be broken easily. Sometimes a cowboy would bring a mouth harp or a harmonica, but guitars, fiddles, and banjos were rare.

Cowboys on a modern trail drive singing around the campfire.

Both cowboy movies and modern trail drives have helped foster the misleading image of trail-drive cowboys singing by the campfire. A common scene in cowboy movies—especially those of the singing cowboys—portrays a lonesome cowboy singing a forlorn song, accompanying himself on guitar or harmonica. Modern trail drives, especially those held on dude ranches, often include singing by the campfire as part of the experience.

■ Why were the trail drives so dangerous?

Trail drives involved months of hard work driving cattle hundreds of miles across open ranges and being challenged by any number of dangers that threatened the lives of both the cattle and the cowboys.

The greatest fear was of a cattle stampede. All cowboys feared the call to action, "All hands and the cook!" A stampede was such a powerful event, it required the help of all the cowboys, even the cook, who usually tended to only his own work and did not help at all with the cattle. All were called into action for a stampede.

A stampede could start for any number of reasons. Cattle are jittery animals, and the slightest provocation can stampede them. Something as simple as the snap of a twig, a flash of lightning, the flare of a match, a cowboy's sneeze, a coyote's howl, or the rustle of a cowboy turning in his bedroll could start a stampede. Cowboys tell of the rising full moon even starting a stampede.

Texas cowboys trying to stop a stampede caused by a lightning storm in 1881. *Frank Leslie's Illustrated Newspaper*, May 1881.

Cowboys report that a stampede usually starts in silence. The cattle suddenly jump to their feet making no sound at all. Then, in just seconds, the earth starts to rumble, and the cattle are off, bellowing and braying to wake the dead.

Cowboys had to stop the stampede as quickly as possible because of the dangers a stampede held for the cattle. Cows could be trampled under foot or might run off ledges and fall to their death. Also, a cow running for miles could lose as much as 50 pounds, and this weight loss would damage the owner's profit at the railhead.

Stampedes were also very dangerous for cowboys. A stampede at night meant that cowboys were racing to get ahead of the herd in the darkness. It was a good possibility that a horse would trip in a ground hole and throw the rider to the ground to a certain death under the hooves of a thousand running cows.

One interesting cowboy description of a stampede tells of the great heat cowboys felt as they raced alongside the stampeding herd. The friction of the cows' bodies rubbing against each other as they stampeded produced an intense heat the cowboys could feel and generated electrical sparks the cowboys could see. In her book, *Cowboys of the Old West*, Gail Stewart describes this "blistering heat" as part of the cowboy's dangerous life.

Crossing a river was another great danger for both cattle and cowboys. Rivers were unpredictable, and cattle could get confused in the middle of a crossing. Cattle instinctively fear the water, and, when frightened, they would begin to mill in a circle in the middle of the river, and many would drown. The swift currents also carried away the weaker cattle that then had to be rescued.

Because most cowboys could not swim, crossing a river and being thrown from one's horse trying to break up milling cattle was very dangerous. Crossing a river was such a difficult job that cowboys gave one of their greatest compliments for a good cowboy by saying, "He's one to ride the river with."

Quicksand and bog holes were another danger on the trail drive. Cows could get stuck in both, and the cowboys had to pull them out without being pulled down themselves.

Another danger was the threat of attack from both rustlers and Indians. The West was still an untamed land during the trail-drive days. Rustlers were abundant and always on the prowl for an easy theft. Because cattle could be re-branded so easily, rustlers saw an easy source of money in stealing cattle from trail drives, re-branding them, and then selling them.

Indians were also a threat because, at that time, the Plains Indians were still in a final battle for their ancestral homelands. The worst encounters with Indians involved battles. Most of the time, however, cowboys told of having to trade cattle for the right to cross Indian land.

■ How did cowboys stop a stampede?

Cowboys stopped a stampede mainly with crazy, foolhardy courage. At the start of a stampede, "all hands and the cook" would mount their horses and race to the head of the stampede. Shooting their pistols and waving their coats, they would try to get the attention of the cattle at the head of the stampede.

Cowboys would also try to get ahead of the running cows and assume the positions of the lead cows. Then they would try to turn the stampede and get the cattle to begin running in a circle. If they were successful, the cattle would begin running in a circle until they began to tire and would then slow down and mill about until the stampede was over.

Frederic Remington illustration of a cowboy struggling to get in position to turn the lead steers in a stampede. From Theodore Roosevelt's *Ranch Life and the Hunting Trail*, 1888.

Cowboys would then spend hours, even days, searching for and collecting the cattle that had strayed away from the herd. Only after all the cattle had been regathered could they move forward on the trail.

■ What is St. Elmo's fire?

St. Elmo's fire was one of the most fascinating dangers of the trail drive. It is an electrical discharge that produces an eerie, luminous blue flash of light. These flashes, or rolling balls of phosphorescent light that were also called fox fire, would run along the ground and over the cattle.

Cowboys reported seeing St. Elmo's fire sparking off the horns of stampeding cattle and searing their backs. The stampeding cattle ran so tightly packed that the friction from their rubbing hides gave off a heat so intense it would sear a cowboy's face if he were riding too close to the herd. The friction also caused the electrical sparking that cowboys called St. Elmo's fire.

Sailors who saw the electrical sparks rolling up their ship's masts named the sparks St. Elmo's fire after St. Erasmus, the patron saint of sailors.

■ What did cowboys do at the end of the trail drive?

The end of a trail drive was a joyous time for cowboys. After many hard and dangerous months, cowboys were ready for a change.

After delivering the cattle to the railhead, they collected their pay. Their first stop was to a barbershop for a haircut, a shave, and a bath. They threw away all their dirty clothes and bought new ones, including boots.

Then, they would go to a restaurant and eat their first real sit-down meal in months. After cleaning up, buying new clothes, and eating a good meal, the cowboys were ready to celebrate. The rest of their time in town was spent at saloons, drinking, gambling, and visiting with dancing girls.

Another popular pastime was getting all dressed up and having a picture taken at a photographic studio. Many of the portraits that still exist from this time period are cowboy studio portraits.

A cowboy all "duded up" for a portrait photo.

By the end of the celebration, most of the cowboys had spent all of their money and either stayed in town for the winter, or headed back south for next year's trail drive.

■ What was the bunkhouse like?

When cowboys worked for a ranch and were not working on a trail drive, they usually stayed in the ranch's bunkhouse, which was the hired hands' cabin. A simple building, the bunkhouse was made of timber, sod, or stacked stone.

Inside was equally plain. In the crude interior there would be wooden or iron bunks, a table and a few chairs, and a wood or coal pot-bellied stove. Cowboys usually covered the walls with newspaper or magazine pages to seal the cracks. They also hung their horse tack and cowboy gear throughout the bunkhouse.

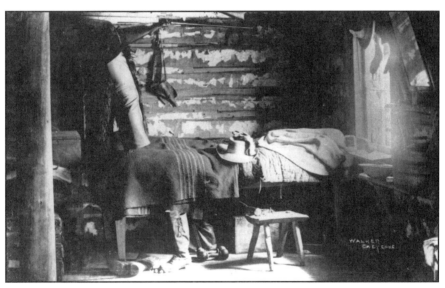

The interior of a bunkhouse in Wyoming.

The ranch owner provided the bunkhouse as living quarters for his ranch hands. The cowboys would spend their free time in the bunkhouse repairing their gear, playing cards, talking, and reading the many horse and cowboy supply catalogues.

■ Were there any Black or Hispanic cowboys on the trail drives?

Even though movies, television, and cowboy fiction present an image of the cowboy that is totally Anglo, the truth is that Black and Hispanic cowboys made up one-third of all the cowboys who rode the trail drives. Black cowboys had worked with cattle in the South during the slave days, and the immense contributions the Spanish and Mexican *vaqueros* made to the establishment of American cowboy culture have been detailed elsewhere in this book.

In the 1820s and 1830s, slaves and Anglo settlers came to Texas and learned *vaquero* skills. By the time of the trail drives forty years later, Anglo, Black, and Hispanic cowboys had worked together for decades on all aspects of cattle work.

Although the actual numbers were never recorded, an estimate cited by Richard Slatta in his book *The Cowboy Encyclopedia* is "63 percent white, 25 percent black, and 12 percent Mexican or Mexican-American cowboys" worked on the trail drives out of Texas from the 1860s to the 1880s.

Two Black cowboys shown at left in Denver, 1900.

While Black and Hispanic cowboys were recognized and respected for their cowboy skills, they never rose to positions of responsibility on the trail drives. Black cowboys, many born slaves, never became ranch foremen or trail bosses because Southerners would not take orders from a Black man. Mexican cowboys, fabled for their horsemanship and roping skills, experienced similar racism. An example of this discrimination is the famous King Ranch in Texas. At the King Ranch, most ranch hands were Mexican *vaqueros*, but all the ranch foremen were Anglo cowboys.

When the trail drives ended, many Black and Hispanic cowboys became western show performers. Their horsemanship, roping, and bronco busting skills made them favorites. Bill Pickett became famous for inventing the sport of bull-dogging. Antonio Esquivel and José "Mexican Joe" Berrara became famous Wild West Show performers for their daredevil equestrian tricks and amazing rope tricks.

Black cowboys created their own rodeos to celebrate and display their cowboy skills. The Bill Pickett Invitational Rodeo and the Black Rodeo of Harlem are two modern rodeos featuring the cowboy skills of Black cowboys.

Cowboys at the second rodeo of the Colored Rodeo Association of Denver.

See pages 106, 108, and 111 in Chapter 5, "Important Cowboys" section for additional information on famous Black cowboys.

■ Were there any cowgirls on the trail drives?

The world of the trail drives was basically a man's world, and almost no women were included. While the history of the West is filled with the contributions of women, the history of the trail drive does not include many of them. Legendary western women such as Calamity Jane, Belle Starr, and Annie Oakley lived lives any man would envy, but the legends of their exploits were not made on the trail drive.

Women populated the West as wives or daughters of cattlemen, but not as hired cattle workers. The realities of nineteenth-century cattle work had men doing all the work with cattle, and women working with cattle from within the confines of a ranch family. Women did work with cattle, but they did it only if they belonged to a ranch family. Most women working cattle were farm girls, not trail-driving cowgirls.

The Becker sisters branding a cow, circa 1894.

Molly Goodnight, wife of Charles Goodnight, rode the trail to Dodge City at least twice. Mrs. D.M. Barton, Belle Barton, wife of Texas cattleman Doc Martin, rode the trail with her husband. Mrs. George Glick, a rancher's wife from Texas, also rode on her husband's trail drives.

One woman who made her own way on the trail drives was Elizabeth E. Johnson. Johnson, a schoolteacher in Texas in the 1870s, wrote romance stories and used the money from her stories to bankroll her life as a rancher. She acquired land, owned cattle, registered her own brand, and drove her own herd up the Chisholm Trail.

The Wild West Shows provided performing opportunities for cowgirls just as they did for cowboys. The most famous woman performer, of course, was Annie Oakley. While most women in the Wild West Shows were not featured performers as Oakley was, women were regular performers and had the opportunity to showcase their cowgirl skills.

Duffy, Della Ferrell, Wild West Show performer.

Women had very important roles in the early history of the rodeo. Rodeo stars such as Lucille Mulhall competed directly against men and became rodeo champions. Mary Lou LeCompte's *Cowgirls of the Rodeo*, Judy Crandall's *Cowgirls, Early Images and Collectibles,* and Candace Savage's *Cowgirls* all give excellent coverage of women's roles in the development of the West and the early days of the rodeo.

Peggy Long, rodeo bronc rider.

See page 17 in Chapter 1 for additional photographs of women rodeo stars.

Riding Into the Sunset

The End of the Trail for the Cowboy

■ Why did the trail drives stop?

The era of the trail drive ended because of many historical forces, and it ended very abruptly. Quite suddenly, in just a few years, the glory days were over.

The first blow came in 1874 when Joseph Glidden patented barbed wire. The most popular legend about its invention is that Glidden's wife asked him to put up a fence to keep dogs out of her garden. Glidden made wire strands with short pieces of twisted, pointed wire wrapped around it. This barbed wire worked very effectively.

At first, farmers and ranchers were wary of barbed wire because they felt it would harm the cattle's hide. Demonstrations proved that it would contain the cattle without harming them. Soon farmers and ranchers throughout the West were using the inexpensive barbed wire to fence their lands. Glidden advertised the wire as "the finest fence in the world, light as air, stronger than whisky, cheaper than dirt." It was nicknamed "the Devil's hat band." By 1880, Glidden was producing 80 million pounds of barbed wire a year.

Adopting barbed wire as a fencing material quickly closed the open ranges. Cattle could no longer be set free to roam and graze. More important, by closing

Barbed wire.

the open ranges, the open paths of the trail drives no longer existed.

In the 1880s, a cattle boom on the northern plains resulted in over-crowding and over-grazing, further stressing the cattle industry. The fertile grasslands of the plains became too depleted to sustain large herds of cattle.

A third sign of trouble for the trail drives was an over supply of beef that saturated the beef market in 1885. With less demand for beef, prices fell, profits declined, and cowboys drove fewer cattle to market.

Several severe weather events further weakened the cattle industry. In 1885, a fierce blizzard killed many cattle. The blizzard of '85 was followed by the drought of '86. Finally, just when the cowboys thought the weather could not get any worse, the blizzards of '86 and '87 decimated herds throughout the West. Many herds lost as much as 70 to 90 percent of their cattle.

Next, a new breed of cattle, a cross between the longhorn and the heavier, short-horned Hereford cow made the longhorn undesirable as a beef cow. The new breed carried more weight, was hardier, and was able to withstand winter cold better. Also, the Texas longhorn took ten years to reach its mature weight of 1,200 pounds. New breeds grew more quickly and were more profitable in less time.

The final blow to the trail drive industry was the completion of the railroad system throughout the West. With railyards close to the cattle herds, it was no longer necessary to drive the cattle long distances to get them to market.

NEW MEXICO—COWBOYS IN THE TEETH OF THE BLIZZARD.—(See page 6.)
DRAWN BY E. J. MEEKER.

New Mexico cowboys in the teeth of the blizzard.

■ What happened to the cowboys after the trail drives stopped?

When the trail drives ended, cowboys throughout the West were out of work. Many tried to find work on western ranches. They hired on as ranch hands and did work they formerly thought no self-respecting cowboy would ever do. They tended winter herds and helped feed cattle. They broke ice on frozen ponds. They pulled cows out of spring bogs. They "rode mill" fixing windmills. They "rode line" fixing fences. Those unable to find regular work on a ranch did "grub line riding," where they rode from ranch to ranch working in exchange for food.

Some left cowboy work, moved to small western towns, and found work as shopkeepers, saloon owners, and hotel workers. Some cowboys became sheepherders, homesteaders, ranchers, or farmers. Others joined the army or became prospectors.

A few lucky cowboys hired on with Wild West Shows, thrilling audiences with exhibitions of cowboy skills and re-enactments of cowboy adventures. Many found the beginnings of the rodeo a substitute for cowboy work.

For most, however, a way of life had ended forever.

FIXING A BREAK IN THE WIRE FENCE

A Frederic Remington illustration of cowboys fixing a break in a wire fence.

■ Are there any real cowboys left?

Yes and no.

In the strict sense of the word, there are no real cowboys left, and there have not been any real cowboys in America for over a century. The era of the real cowboy, the cowboy who made American history and was the source of the cowboy myth, was very short. The time of the traditional cowboy, who drove cattle on the trail drives, was from the mid-1860s to the mid-1880s, a mere 20 years. When the trail drives ended, the work of the real cowboy ended also.

If the definition of a cowboy is simply a horseman who works with cattle, however, then there are real, hard-working cowboys on every ranch in America today. Today's cowboys use trucks, jeeps, helicopters, and computers to do their work, but they wear a cowboy outfit very similar to the one worn over 100 years ago. They are as proud of their hats and boots as any cowboy ever was. They listen to country music, and they try to live by a cowboy code of honor. Most important, since clothes and music alone do not make a real cowboy, they still have the traditional cowboy skills of "ridin', ropin' and branding." And they would be insulted if anyone said they were not real cowboys. The modern ranch worker believes he is as real a cowboy as there ever was.

Today's rodeos also provide opportunities for cowboys and cowgirls to display their skills before appreciative audiences. Rodeo performers consider themselves to be real cowboys and their ropin' and ridin' skills are as good as any cowboy who ever rode the trail.

Rodeo cowboy performing a rope trick on horseback.

Cowboy Wisdom

Expert Facts About Cowboys

■ What cowboy words came from the Spanish language?

At one time, the cowboy's language was Spanish only. During the *vaquero* period, the Spanish/Mexican cowboy gave names to many of the cowboy practices. When the American settlers came into Texas in the early to mid-1800s, they adopted the *vaquero* vocabulary as they learned the *vaquero* ways of handling vast herds on the open plains of southern Texas. Many of these terms are still used today by cowboys and ranch workers. Following is a list of common cowboy words and practices derived from the Spanish language and Spanish/Mexican *vaquero* traditions.

Armas: tough leather flaps on saddle sides, derived from *armar*, Spanish for to arm or strengthen

Armitas: chinks (short chaps) or leather apron, derived from armar

Bosal: a muzzle or harness over a horse's nose, derived from *bozal*, Spanish for muzzle

Botas: leather or buckskin leggings

Bronco: rough horse, derived from *bronco caballo*

Buckaroo: cowboy slang for bronco rider, derived from *vaquero*

Caballero: gentleman horse rider

Chaps: leather leggings, derived from *chaparreras* or *chaparejos*, also from *chaparro prieto*, thistle or thorn bush

Cinch: saddle strap, derived from *cincha*, Spanish for girth

Concho: a decorative disk-like holder on saddles and leather gear, from *conch*, Spanish for shell

Corona: saddle blanket, Spanish for crown

Corral: yard or enclosure, Spanish for stockyard

Dally: loose tying of rope over saddle horn, derived from *dar la vuelta*, Spanish for to give a turn

Hackamore: rope harness over a horse's nose, no bit in the mouth, derived from *jáquima*

Honda: end of rope loop on the lariat, Spanish for sling or rope used for hoisting

Hoosegow: cowboy slang for jail, derived from *juzgado*, Spanish for court-room

Jerky: dried strips of meat, derived from *charquí*, strips of meat dried in the sun, also from *charquear*, Spanish for to cut into pieces

Jinete: horse breaker, Spanish for horseman

Ladinos: runaway, stray, outlaw cattle, Spanish for crafty or sly

Lariat: rope, derived from *la reata*, Spanish for rope

Lasso: rope, derived from *lazo*, Spanish for snare or trap

McCarty: horsehair rope, derived from *mecate*

Mustang: wild horse, derived from *mesteño*, strays from the *Mesta*, the Spanish organization of cattle and horse owners

Poblano: *vaquero* hat, low crown, and wide brim

Quirt: short hand whip, derived from *cuerda* (or *cuarta*) *de cordón*, Spanish for whip or cord

Ranch: variation of *rancho*

Reatero: Spanish for rope maker

Remuda: extra horses for the trail drivers, Spanish for exchange, remount

Remudero: horse wrangler, caretaker of the *remuda*

Rodeo: roundup, derived from *rodear*, Spanish for to surround

Romal: longer reins serving as a quirt, derived from *ramal*, Spanish for halter

Sombrero: *vaquero* hat, derived from *sombra*, Spanish for shade

Stampede: wild running of cattle, derived from *estampida*, Spanish for explosions or crash

Sudadero: leather saddle fenders to keep horse's sweat off rider's legs, derived from *sudar*, Spanish for to sweat

Tapaderos: leather stirrup covers, derived from *tapar*, Spanish for to cover

Ten-gallon Hat: high-crowned cowboy hat, derived from *tan galan*, Spanish for very fine

Vaquero: Spanish/Mexican cowboy, derived from *vaca*, Spanish for cow

Wrangler: a stableman, horse trainer, derived from *caballerango*

■ What are the cowboy words and terms I should know?

Like any specialized activity, the world of cowboys and ranch workers has its own language and vocabulary. As noted in the previous section, many of these words came from the Spanish language of the first cowboys, the Spanish/Mexican *vaqueros*. This cowboy glossary is divided into five categories to help you better learn the names and terms cowboys use to describe their world and their work.

Of course, there are many more cowboy terms than are listed here. In addition, many terms are regional or personal and are not used by all cowboys; but the terms listed here are ones you should know to have a beginner's working vocabulary and understanding of the cowboy world.

Cowboy Jobs

Boss Man: owner of the ranch

Bronc Buster: a cowboy who breaks wild horses

Brush Popper: a cowboy who rides into the thick brush to search for hidden cows

Buckaroo: a cowboy from the western states, usually California or Oregon

Caballero: a Spanish gentleman who rides and deals in horses

Cattleman: a man who owns, raises, and sells cows

Charro: Spanish or Mexican horseman

Cookie: the chuck wagon cook on a trail drive, usually an older or retired cowboy

Cow Boss: the cowboy in charge of running the ranch, usually in charge of hiring and firing the working cowboys and assigning the cowboys their jobs

Cow Puncher: a nickname for a cowboy (cow punchers would use long poles to poke or punch cows into ramps leading up to railroad cars on trains)

Dally Man: a cowboy who loosely wraps his rope around the saddle horn when roping a cow

Drag Rider: the cowboy who rides at the back end of the trail drive, the hardest and dirtiest job on a trail drive

Drover: a cowboy who works on the trail drive

Flank Rider: the cowboy who rides at the side of the herd, behind the swing riders, to help keep the herd together and heading in the correct direction

Horseman: a cowboy who rides and tends to horses

Lead Riders: the cowboys who ride at the front of the trail drive by the lead cattle, leading the herd in the proper direction

Night Herders: the cowboys who circle the herd at night, keeping the herd safe and contained

Night Wrangler: the cowboy who tends to the saddle horses at night

Point Rider: the cowboy who rides in front of the herd leading the whole cattle drive in the correct direction

Pool Rider: a cowboy who works for several ranchers

Rancher: a person who owns or works cattle on a ranch

Rustler: a cattle thief

Swing Rider: the cowboys who ride at the side of the herd, in front of the flank riders, helping to keep the herd together and heading in the correct direction

Tally Man: the cowboy who keeps the records, or tallies, of the cows on the trail drive or at the ranch; he also keeps a record of the cows' brands and ear marks

Tenderfoot: an inexperienced newcomer

Tie Man: a cowboy who fast-ties his rope to the saddle horn when roping a cow

Top Hand: usually the ranch foreman

Trail Boss: the cowboy in charge of the trail drive; he rode at the front of the trail drive and would scout for the correct trail and places to water the herd and settle for the night

Waddie: an extra cowboy who fills in

Wrangler: another name for a working cowboy, especially one who tends to the saddle horses

Cowboy Gear (see pictures and illustrations in chapter 2)

Bedroll: a large canvas tarp used like a sleeping bag by cowboys

Boots: high-topped, pointed-toe, raked-heel boots specialized for cowboy work. The high tops protect the cowboy's legs; the pointed toes slide easily into the stirrups, and the raked heel secures the boot heel into the stirrup.

Chaps: protective leather leggings worn by cowboys

Chaps, Shotgun: tight-fitting chaps that wrap around the leg and are put on like pants

Chaps, Bat-wing: loose fitting chaps that just wrap around the legs

Chaps, Woolies: wool-covered chaps used in cold weather; also called angora chaps if made from Angora goat hair

Chinks: short-legged chaps, usually reaching just below the knee

Cuffs: leather wristband used for arm protection

Jingle Bobs: metal balls attached to the back of the spur to hit the rowels and make a ringing sound cowboys enjoy

Outfit: general term for a cowboy's equipment and clothes

Rawhide: unprocessed and untanned cowhide with abundant uses for cowboy equipment

Rope: the primary cowboy tool, made of braided horse hair, Manila hemp, braided or twisted rawhide, or Mexican cactus

Rowel: the spinning, disk-like metal points attached to the spur shaft at the rear of the spur

Quirt: short, leather braided whip

Slicker: waterproof long coat used in foul weather

Sombrero: a large-brimmed Mexican cowboy hat

Spurs: metal U-shaped devices attached to the boot heel; used to spur the horse to speed up

Stampede String: the leather chin strap on a cowboy hat

Tally Book: a small notebook used to record the number of cattle at a roundup

Teepee: a small canvas tent used by cowboys when camping on the range

Warbag: a cloth bag that held most of a cowboy's personal possessions

Wildrag: a nickname for a cowboy's bandana

Horse Terms

Bay: a brown or reddish-brown horse with a black mane, tail, and lower legs

Bell Mare: an older mare wearing a bell, used as lead horse in a pack train or in a *remuda* to help locate where the horses are grazing at night

Bronco: a wild, unbroken horse

Broom-tail: a horse cowboys do not think is worth very much

Buckskin: a yellow-colored horse with a black mane and tail

Cavvy: the horses selected from the *remuda* to be the work horses for the day

Cavyard: the *remuda* or horse herd

Cayuse: a range-bred horse, horses descended from mustangs, a wild horse

Chestnut: a brown or reddish-brown horse

Colt: a young horse; technically, a stallion less than a year old

Cow Horse: a horse that is trained to work with cowboys in roping, cutting, and herding cows

Cow Sense: the natural ability of a horse to work with cattle

Cutting Horse: a horse that is trained to work with the cowboy at a roundup for cutting cows away from the herd for roping and branding

Filly: a young female horse

Flaxie: blond-colored mane or tail on a horse

Hurricane Deck: the saddle on a bucking horse

Mare: a female horse

Mustang: a wild, unbroken horse

Off-side: the right side of a horse; the side you don't mount on. The reason a rider mounts from the left side has many explanations. The most common is that most people are right-handed and in past times, soldiers mounted horses from the left because they had to mount horses while wearing a sword. Since the sword hung on their left side, it was much easier to mount with the sword hanging freely on the leg, rather than trying to swing it up over the back of the horse. Nowadays, a well-trained horse will let a rider mount from either side, but we still use the left side most of the time.

Paint: a spotted horse

Palomino: a golden-colored horse with a light-colored mane and tail

Pinto: a spotted or painted horse

Quarter Horse: a horse noted for high speed and agility over short distances, especially favored for cowboy and ranch work

Remuda: all the saddle work horses on a trail drive

Rough Sting: a horse that always bucks when saddled

Sorrel: a reddish-colored horse

Stray: a lost horse, separated from its owner or home range

Stallion: an adult male horse

Wheel Team: the first team attached to the wagon when more than one team is needed to pull the wagon

Widow Maker: an especially ill-tempered horse

Horse Gear (also called tack)

Bridle: the term used to describe the complete horse head harness consisting of the headstall, bit, chin strap, and reins; often also including a brow band, nose strap, and throat latch

Bridle.

Bit: a metal mouthpiece inserted into the horse's mouth, connected to the reins, to guide and control the horse

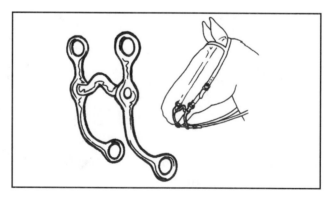

Bit.

Bosal: the noseband part of a hackamore (see below), a bit-less headpiece used to train young horses

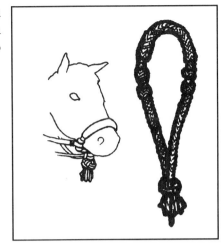

Bosal.

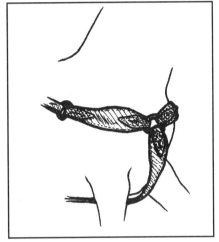

Breast Collar.

Breast Collar: a leather strap that passes around the horse's chest and is attached to the saddle so it does not slide backward

Cinch: a leather or fabric belt on the saddle that is tightened abound the horse's belly to keep the saddle secure. A double-rigged cinch has two belts, one in front and one behind the saddle seat. A single-cinch saddle has just one belt, usually more centered on the saddle.

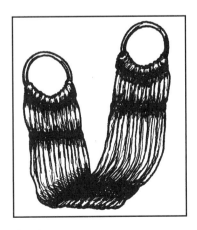

Cinch.

Cinch Ring: the rings at the end of the cinch used for securing the saddle to the horse with the cinch straps

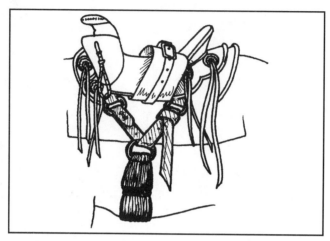

Cinch Ring.

Hackamore: a bit-less headpiece, usually of leather or rope, fitting over the horse's nose and head, used to train young horses before they go on the bit. Some traditional cowboys believe a hackamore-trained horse is better than a bit-trained horse because the hackamore is a gentler and better way to control and guide a horse. Talking about this is a good way to start an argument among cowboys.

Hackamore.

Halter: a headstall (see below) with an attached rope for holding and leading a horse

Headstall: straps that go over a horse's head, which, together with the bit and the reins, form the bridle

Hobbles: short straps placed around a horse's ankles to restrict movement

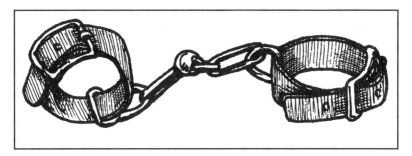

Hobbles.

McCarty: a rope, often of braided horsehair, used as a combination rein and lead rope

Morral: a feedbag that fits over a horse's nose

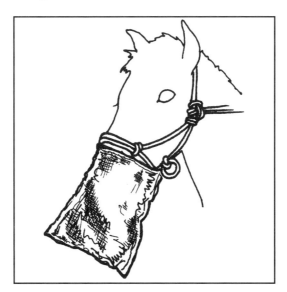

Morral.

Rein: the straps connected to the bridle that the cowboy uses to control the horse

Saddle: a leather-covered horse-riding seat for the cowboy (see figures on pages 32 and 34)

Saddle Blanket: a thick blanket or pad put under the saddle to protect the horse

Saddle Bags: leather or canvas bags used to carry extra gear on the saddle

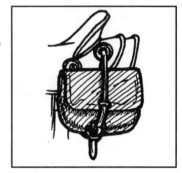

Saddle Bag.

Soogan: the quilt or comforter in a cowboy's bedroll

Tapaderos: also called taps, leather foot protectors attached to the front of the stirrups (see figures on page 35)

Cattle Terms

Beeves: steers over three years old

Bull: a male uncastrated bovine

Calf: a baby cow

Cow: a female bovine

Dogie: a calf with no mother. The word *dogie* refers to cattle; not to dogs. It is pronounced with a long *o*, as in row. Cowboy lore gives two versions as to the origin of *dogie*. One refers to a motherless calf that had to eat grass before being able to digest it. This caused the calf's stomach to swell, which cowboys referred to as "dough guts," which became "dogie." The other story says that the term came from the Spanish word *dogal*, meaning a short rope halter used to keep a calf away from its mother while she was being milked.

Heifer: a young female cow who has not borne a calf

Hereford: a breed of beef cattle with rust-colored coats and white faces

Leppy: an orphan calf; same as a dogie

Longhorn: the primary cattle of the trail drives; descended from Spanish cattle, they were large, muscular and hardy cattle, well suited for the long and often harsh trail drives; characterized by their long, up to 8- or 9-foot, horns

Maverick: a wild, unbranded cow

Mossy: a renegade steer

Shelly cow: an old cow in poor condition

Steer: a castrated bovine

■ What are some cowboy sayings?

Cowboys were known for their unique way with language. Like any select group of workers, they had a specialized language to describe their work and themselves and to express their feeling about their life experiences. Even though the American cowboy has the image of being strong and silent, with the emphasis on silent, the words he does say live in history as some of the most expressive ever spoken. Even today, modern ranch hands, rodeo performers, and western people continue to use cowboy language to express themselves. This cowboy lingo can be as simple as a single, but descriptive word, or as evolved as the metaphor-filled expressions of cowboy poetry. Whatever it is, short or long, the American English language has been enriched by the wit and wisdom of cowboy language. Here are a few examples of the picturesque and colorful cowboy sayings.

1. *He rides tall in the saddle.* A compliment said of a first-rate, righteous, top-hand cowboy.

2. *I can tell by your outfit you're a cowboy.* Only a true cowboy would have all the correct gear.

3. *He likes to change hats.* Said of someone who keeps changing from good to bad.

4. *Don't squat with your spurs on.* A warning to be careful and stay aware at all times.

5. *You bet your boots.* You are so right.

6. *He sold his saddle.* Said of a man who had left the cowboy profession.

7. *Head 'em up, ride 'em out.* Encouraging command yelled at the start of the day's trail drive.

8. *He's just a spud/tenderfoot.* Said of a fresh, young cowboy.

9. *Can't see to can't see.* From morning to nighttime.

10. *Hold onto your horses.* Now, just wait a minute.

11. *He'll take the slack out of your rope.* Said of someone who can teach you a lesson.

12. *He's careless with his branding iron.* Said of someone suspected of being a thief.

13. *His cooking tastes like it was made with the cook's socks.* Said of bad cooking.

14. *All hands and the cook.* Command yelled at the start of a stampede for everybody to get going and help stop the stampede.

15. *She's a pistol-packing mama.* Said of a rough and tumble woman.

16. *He's made of rough leather.* Said of a rough and tumble man.

17. *He's my right-hand man.* A compliment. Said of a good, trustworthy and helpful man.

18. *He's up to scratch.* Said of a person who can get the job done.

19. *You don't get lard unless you boil the hog.* You have to work for what you get.

20. *You can spread it around, now let's see what you can do when it's all gathered up.* You can talk a good story but can you back it up.

21. *I saved his bacon.* I saved his life.

22. *Broke his arm patting his own back.* Said of someone who is conceited.

23. *Smells like a shot-up barbershop.* Said of someone who wears too much cologne.

24. *He's knocked out horses.* Said of a tough man.

25. *He couldn't see through a barbed wire fence.* Said of someone who is not too smart.

26. *Running maverick.* Said of someone who is a loner.

27. *Riding shotgun.* Said of someone who is a protector.

28. *He wears a white hat.* A good cowboy.

29. *He wears a black hat.* A bad cowboy.

30. *Watching the op'ra.* Sitting on the top rail of the corral. The top rail was known as the opry house.

31. *Range delivery.* After the sale of cattle, the buyer had to go out on the range and collect the cows himself.

32. *He's square.* A compliment meant for a righteous, reliable, and able cowboy.

33. *Get off and rest your hat.* An invitation to stay and share a meal.

34. *He's riding the fence.* Said of a cowboy's work of inspecting and repairing the fence line.

35. *He could follow a wood tick on a solid rock in the dark of the moon.* Said of a good tracker.

36. *He couldn't find a calf with a bell on in a corral.* Said of a bad tracker.

37. *He's a chuck line rider.* Said of a cowboy who was out of work and rode through a county depending upon the hospitality of other cowboys.

38. *To roll the cotton.* To roll up the bedroll and prepare it for packing away.

39. *He's strutting like a gobbler at laying time.* Said of a dressed up cowboy.

40. *He's duded up to put on a good hoof.* Said of a dressed up cowboy on his way to a dance.

41. *That rope can sing.* Said of a broken-in rope that hisses when it is thrown properly.

42. *You couldn't throw it into a well.* Said of a bad rope, too stiff to throw.

43. *Waltz with the lady!* An encouraging word yelled to a bronc buster trying to stay on a bucking wild horse.

44. *He's bucking on a dime.* Said of a bucking horse that stays in one spot.

45. *He's a pile driver.* Said of a bucking horse that lands on all four stiff legs.

46. *Hundred and elevens.* Spur marks on a horse's flanks.

47. *Shaking hands with grandma.* Holding onto the saddle horn when riding a bucking horse.

48. *He couldn't ride a covered wagon.* Said of a man who has little riding ability.

49. *Wake up snakes and bite a biscuit.* The cook's yell to come and eat.

50. *He's a saddle blanket gambler.* Said of a man who gambles for small stakes.

51. *He's kicking like a bay steer.* Said of a cowboy who is complaining too much.

52. *He's trying to scratch his ear with his elbow.* Said of a cowboy who is trying to do something impossible.

53. *His family tree was a shrub.* Said of a worthless person.

54. *He don't know dung from wild honey.* Said of a stupid person.

55. *He has to stand twice to make a shadow.* Said of a very thin person.

56. *He's grabbing the branding iron by the hot end.* Said of a cowboy who is taking a chance.

57. *He's one to ride the river with.* A compliment. One of the most difficult and dangerous cowboy jobs was herding cattle across rivers. A cowboy who could do that job was a top cowboy and a good man.

58. *He rides for the brand.* Said of a cowboy who is loyal to his employer.

59. *He just stepped off the trail.* Said of a cowboy who got married or got another job.

60. *He's careful as a naked man climbing a barbed wire fence.* Cowboy expression.

61. *Never kick a fresh cow pie on a hot day.* Cowboy expression.

62. *Trust everybody in the game, but always cut the cards.* Cowboy expression.

63. *Always drink upstream from the herd.* Cowboy expression.

64. *When a cowboy's too old to set a bad example, he hands out good advice.* Cowboy expression.

65. *There's not a horse that can't be broke or a man that can't be thrown.* Cowboy expression.

66. *He's louder than a rusty hinge.* Cowboy insult.

67. *He sounds like a donkey with a bad cold.* Cowboy insult.

68. *He's a skim milk cowboy. (Dresses like a cowboy, but isn't one.)* Cowboy insult.

69. *He can't ride anything wilder than a rocking chair.* Cowboy insult.

70. *You look worse than a calf with the slobbers.* Cowboy insult.

71. *He's never been closer to a cow than a milk wagon.* Cowboy insult.

72. *You draw trouble like an outhouse draws flies.* Cowboy insult.

■ Who are some of the important cowboys and cowgirls?

The history of the West was created by many of America's most brave, adventurous, and wild characters. Every aspect of this history, especially the history of the cowboy, has its heroes and legendary figures. Following are some of the people who played an important role in the history of the cowboy West. Many became famous for their deeds and exploits; many were working cowboys, some were not; but they all made important contributions to the history of the cowboy.

Edward Abbott

(1860–1939) Edward Abbot, nicknamed Teddy Blue Abbot, was a cowboy and rancher. He wrote the book *We Pointed Them North: Recollections of a Cowpuncher.* His book is considered to be one of the best books ever written about cowboy life.

James Beckwourth

(1798–1866) James Beckwourth was an African-American who played a part in the early exploration of the frontier West. The son of a slave and a plantation owner, Beckwourth was a frontiersman, trapper, mountain man, and scout guide. In 1856, Harper and Brothers published his autobiography, *The Life and Adventures of James P. Beckwourth, Mountaineer, Scout, and Pioneer, and Chief of the Crow Nation of Indians.* He spent years living with the Crow Indians and had numerous Indian wives. His greatest contribution to the history of the West occurred in the Sierra Nevada mountains. He had come to California for the gold rush, and he knew that one of the most difficult parts of the journey was crossing the high passes through the Sierra Nevadas. In 1850, he discovered an easier route through the mountains and, in 1851, personally led the first wagon train of settlers through the pass, which is named Beckwourth Pass in his honor.

Calamity Jane

(1852–1903) Calamity Jane's real name was Martha Jane Canary. Although there are several versions of the true origin of her nickname, she was known as a hard-drinking, hard-living woman who dressed like a man, cussed like a man, and worked like a man. She grew up in mining camps and rough frontier communities. She was a frontier woman who bragged that she could shoot with the best of men. She claimed to have been a gold miner, a nurse, a Pony Express rider, an army scout, an Indian fighter, and a cattle hand. She became famous when the exploits of her life appeared in several dimestore pulp novels. In her later years, she appeared in the Wild West Shows. She supposedly secretly married Wild Bill Hickok and had a child with him in 1873. Her life ended sadly; her eyesight was failing and she was broke. She is buried in Deadwood, Dakota Territory, next to Wild Bill Hickok.

Jesse Chisholm

(1806–1868) Jesse Chisholm was a frontier scout, guide, hunter, trader, and pathfinder. Half Scottish and half Cherokee Indian, he lived with the Cherokee tribes as a youth. He later ran trading posts in Oklahoma. He knew a number of Indian languages and successfully traded with the Oklahoma and Kansas tribes. He was often called upon to interpret for the Indians. He became known as the

"Peacemaker of the Plains" because of his diplomatic skills at negotiating conflicts between Indians and white settlers, as well as between Indian tribes. His trading took him south of Wichita, Kansas, to the North Canadian River in Oklahoma and Texas. It was this wagon freight trail that later became a main trail used by the cowboys to bring their cattle to the Kansas cow towns. The trail became known as the Chisholm Trail and was one of the primary routes of the great trail drives.

William F. Cody

(1846–1917) William F. Cody, better known as Buffalo Bill, lived one of the most exciting lives of the cowboy frontier. At various times in his life, he was a frontiersman, a Pony Express rider, a Civil War soldier, a scout, an actor, a buffalo hunter, and a showman. He earned his nickname, Buffalo Bill, by shooting buffalo to supply meat for the workers on the Kansas Pacific Railroad. Novelist Ned Buntline, who wrote exciting dimestore novels with Buffalo Bill as the hero, shaped Buffalo Bill's legend as a frontier hero. His greatest fame was as the producer of the world-famous Wild West Shows. Cody presented his shows as an exciting spectacle in which audiences could see an authentic portrayal of rugged frontier life. In 1882, he organized his first show featuring rodeo and horseback competitions. His shows later developed into vast extravaganzas featuring real Indians, sharpshooting riders, and Mexican *vaquero* rope-trick experts. The show was so successful that it played at world's fairs throughout America and on the European continent. Queen Victoria of England so enjoyed the show that she requested an encore performance. Cody, through his astute showmanship and his epic life as a frontier hero, is largely responsible for the grand myth of the cowboy as we know it today.

William Cody, 1889.

Elizabeth Collins

(1844–1921) Elizabeth Collins, also known as Libby Smith Collins, was the first woman to ship cattle from Montana to Chicago. She first came west with her parents in the 1850s. She had many western adventures, including being captured by Indians, before she and her husband, Nat Collins, settled down on a small ranch with 180 head of cattle. She and her husband worked a ranch near Choteau, Montana. One year her husband fell sick and was unable to take their cattle to Chicago for sale. At that time, the railroad prohibited women from accompanying stock on a cattle train; they couldn't even ride the train, even if they paid full fare. Elizabeth, however, persevered and eventually was granted a special permit to accompany her cattle to Chicago on the train. Legend has it that as she boarded the train, the cowboys cheered her on and yelled out "Success to Aunty Collins, the Cattle Queen of Montana." In Chicago, she sold her cattle and, after that experience, often took the cattle to Chicago herself. Newspapers and magazines wrote about her story as a woman taking care of the family's business matters. In the 1950s, a movie was made about her called *Cattle Queen of Montana*, starring Barbara Stanwyck and Ronald Reagan.

Isom Dart

(1849–1900) Isom Dart's life was a combination of great successes and terrible tragedy. His original name was Ned Huddleston, and he was born a slave in Arkansas. He escaped slavery, and at age 16 he moved to Texas after the emancipation of the slaves. He traveled to Mexico and became a stunt rider. Returning to the United States, he worked as a bronc buster and became known as a great horseman. Dart's life, however, became a life of crime as he joined up with some horse rustlers. He had several close calls with the law, eventually changing his name to Isom Dart to escape capture. He eventually bought a ranch and tried to live a

Isom Dart.

law-abiding life hunting and breaking wild horses, but his past eventually caught up with him. In 1900, bounty hunter Tom Horn, whose job it was to hunt down ex-horse rustlers, shot and killed Dart in cold blood as he walked out of his cabin. Dart's life was an example of how a life in the cowboy West could contain both the good and the bad.

Charles Goodnight

(1836–1929) In 1856, Charles Goodnight entered the cattle business in the northwest Texas frontier. His enterprise, however, was interrupted by the Civil War. After the war, Goodnight returned to Texas and resurrected his business. His primary concern was how to get his cattle to market outside of the war-ravaged South. He decided upon a path through west Texas and New Mexico, up into Colorado. With his partner, an older rancher named Oliver Loving, Goodnight pioneered this new trail, which cowboys called the Goodnight-Loving Trail. Over the years, the Goodnight-Loving Trail became one of the most heavily traveled in the Southwest. Goodnight is also known as the inventor of the chuck wagon. Needing to feed his trail drivers, he modified an old army wagon to feed his crews. Previously, cowboys had each brought their own food on the trail drives.

Prairie Rose Henderson

(?–1930s) Prairie Rose Henderson was a pioneer female rodeo entertainer. Her exact birth date has never been known. She was born Ann Robbins anywhere from the 1870s to 1890. Her name, Prairie Rose, supposedly came from the Wyoming prairie, and Henderson was her first husband's name. She was known for her colorful and flashy outfits, many with fancy beaded leather and even feathers and sequins. She began riding in 1906, eventually being declared one of the all-time great champion winners, excelling as a bronc rider. By 1911, she had been awarded the title of Champion; and in 1917, the Union Pacific Railroad awarded her the Championship Silver Buckle for bronc riding. Her death was as clouded as her birth. In the 1930s, she left her ranch house in a blizzard, possibly to tend to some lost animals, and she never returned. Years later her body was found and was identified by her large championship silver belt buckle.

Wild Bill Hickok

(1837–1876) Wild Bill Hickok was one of the frontier's most notorious gunmen and lawmen. His exploits as a gunman often involved gamblers and drunken cowboys and ended in the shooting death of his victims. As a U.S. marshal, he often shot first and asked questions later when stopping a western town's battles. His fame grew as newspaper reporters exaggerated and embellished the facts of his life and helped create the legendary stories of Wild Bill Hickok for national audiences. He lived by the gun, and he died by the gun. In 1876, in Deadwood, Dakota Territory, at Saloon No. 10, he was shot in the back and killed during a poker game.

Captain Richard King

(1824–1885) Richard King was the founder of the most famous ranch of all time, the Texas King Ranch. In his early life, King was a Gulf Coast river boatman, eventually working his way up to the position of captain. His title of captain referred to his boating experiences and was not a military reference. From 1850 until the Civil War, King built a steamship company that did an immense trade in cotton. In 1853, King traveled through southern Texas and realized that a great future lay in land and cattle. Using the wealth from his steamship company, he purchased 15,500 acres of land between the Nueces River and the Rio Grande, a holding that would grow to 600,000 acres by his death in 1885. King hired Mexican *vaqueros* to maintain both the cattle herds and the ranch. These *vaqueros* became well-known for their skills and loyalty to the King Ranch. Through the following generations, his family continued to expand the ranch, and it is the acknowledged birthplace of the American ranching industry. The ranch has developed two major cattle breeds and performance horses and is a source of ranching practices that have led to many significant advances in livestock and wildlife production and management.

Nat Love

(1854–1921) Nat Love, a former slave, was a renowned African-American cowboy who helped created his own myth. His autobiography, published in 1907, had an extravagant title: *The Life and Adventures of Nat Love, Better Known in the Cattle Country as "Deadwood Dick," by Himself; a True History of Slavery Days, Life on the Great Cattle Ranges and on the Plains of the "Wild and Woolly" West, Based on Facts, and Personal Experiences of the Author.* It was filled with exploits that read like tall tales, depicting Indian fights, beautiful maidens, and famous outlaws. He also claimed to be the real Deadwood Dick, the real-life cowboy whose life was depicted in the popular pulp-novel series of the time, *Deadwood Dick*, written by Edward Wheeler. He often told the story of how he received the nickname Deadwood Dick, by winning roping and shooting contests in Deadwood City in the Dakota Territory. He was a true trail cowboy, working the cattle drives on the Chisholm Trail, and he became the most famous African-American cowboy of all time.

Nat Love, "In my fighting clothes."

Oliver Loving

(1812–1867) Oliver Loving was known as the "Dean of the Trail Drivers, " a title he earned by driving cattle on long, difficult trail drives through territory no one had ever traveled before. Many of the trail drives undertaken by Loving occurred before the days of the great trail drives. Some of his first drives were to Louisiana. In 1858, he took the first herd of Texas longhorns to a northern market, all the way to Illinois. Loving also realized that cattle markets existed in Colorado, and, in 1860, he drove a herd to Denver, the first herd of Texas longhorns to reach Colorado. After the Civil War, he realized that the cattle drives traveling to north Texas would be overcrowded. Capitalizing on his previously successful drive to Colorado, he took another herd to Colorado in 1866 with his partner, Charles Goodnight. Traveling along a trail west across south Texas, into New Mexico, and then north to Colorado, he established the famous Goodnight-Loving Trail.

Joseph McCoy

(1837–1915) Joseph McCoy was the "father of the cow town." He convinced the railroads that building stockyards near western rail lines was good business. He then built his stockyards near Abilene, Kansas, and sent word to Texans about his rail yards. In just a few years, more than a million head of cattle were being driven to his rail yards. He turned Abilene into the first of the famous cow towns.

Lucille Mulhall

(1855–1949) The following is quoted from the book jacket of *America's First Cowgirl: Lucille Mulhall*, by Beth Day. "World's Champion Roper—America's Greatest Horsewoman—Queen of the Range—and the only woman who ever roped steers competitively with men—Lucille Mulhall held the top spot in contests and vaudeville for twenty years. Will Rogers, friend and teacher, called her 'the world's greatest rider.' " Lucille Mulhall is often called "America's First Cowgirl." The daughter of Zach Mulhall, founder of the Mulhall Wild West Shows, she was the first lady to be called a cowgirl. Legend has it that Will Rogers himself first called her a cowgirl after he saw her first public performance in 1899 winning her father's roping and riding contest. In the Wild West Shows she was billed as the "Champion Lady Rider and Roper of the World." She competed in rodeos and performed in Wild West Shows into the 1940s. In 1975 she was inducted into the Rodeo Hall of Fame.

Annie Oakley

(1860–1926) Annie Oakley, one of the most famous women in the legend of the Old West, was a sharpshooting superstar in Buffalo Bill Cody's Wild West Shows. For 17 years, she traveled the world with the shows, thrilling audiences with her legendary shooting. She hit moving targets on foot, on horseback, even on bicycles. She shot with both hands and from behind her back. She could shoot a dime out of a man's hand, split a card in two at 30 paces, hit coins and glass balls tossed into the air, and shoot a cigarette out of a

Annie Oakley, "Little Sure Shot."

man's mouth. One of her most famous tricks was hitting targets while shooting backward, looking through a mirror to see the target. She was immensely popular with audiences, and she became the top attraction in the Wild West Shows. Sioux chief Sitting Bull nicknamed her "Little Sure Shot." Her life story is told in the famous Broadway musical *Annie Get Your Gun.*

Lulu Belle Parr

(1876–1955) Lulu Belle Parr was the first famous female bronc rider. She was one of the earliest and prettiest female rodeo contestants. In the 1890s, she gained fame as a champion bronc and steer rider. She then left the rodeo circuit to become a full-time performer in the Wild West Shows. Between 1910 and 1920, she was a headliner with the Buffalo Bill, Pawnee Bill, and 101 Wild West Shows. She remained an active performer well into middle age.

Bill Pickett

(1870–1932) Bill Pickett is the most famous Black rodeo performer of all time. In 1971, he became the first African-American inducted into the National Cowboy Hall of Fame. Today, the nation's only touring African-American rodeo is named the Bill Pickett Invitational Rodeo. Bill Picket is credited with inventing the rodeo sport of bulldogging, or steer wrestling. He first demonstrated his technique of stopping a steer by biting its lips to a group of cowboys in 1881. He claimed to have seen a bulldog bring a steer to a stop by biting its lips and adopted the strategy himself. In 1994, the United States Postal Service honored him by issuing a commemorative stamp of him in its Legends of the West series.

Bill Pickett.

Frederic Remington

(1861–1909) Frederic Remington was America's most renowned western artist and played a primary role in providing America with its images of western and cowboy life. His illustrations of cowboys and cowboy life are historical documents, giving us instructive images and knowledge of a past American era. These are the images that helped create the wonderful American myth of the rugged cowboy at work. Remington's art training was traditional and formal. He attended Yale University in the School of Fine Arts and the New York Arts Art Students League. In 1881, he took a trip to the West and realized the possibilities and need of documenting the cowboy's life artistically. Even though he spent his adult life living in New York, he made frequent trips to the West to fuel his artistic imagination and work. He became a popular and successful illustrator for magazines, especially *Harper's Weekly.* He became one of the most famous and successful illustrators in America. Today, he is known for his vast output of illustrations covering the vanishing American West. He is especially recognized for the careful authenticity he brought to his illustrations. Legend holds that at his death he cried out, "Cowboys! There are no cowboys anymore."

Will Rogers

(1879–1935) Will Rogers was America's most famous cowboy during the 1920s and 1930s. Born in Oklahoma, the son of a rancher, he became an expert trick roper. His early fame came in the Wild West Shows where he performed as a rope artist and bronc buster. He found international fame with his act performing rope tricks while adding political humor and wisecracks in his western drawl. He later moved to Hollywood, where he worked successfully in the movies and also became a nationally syndicated newspaper political columnist. He was beloved for his easy-going personality, admired for his trick rope artistry, and respected for his "common sense, common man" perspective on social and political events. He was America's "Cowboy

Will Rogers.

Philosopher." Cowboy fans can enjoy his legendary roping skills in the silent film *The Roping Fool.*

Charles Russell

(1864–1926) Charles Russell, along with Frederic Remington, was one of America's most famous western artists. He is often referred to as the "Cowboy Artist of the West." Russell had no formal training in the arts. He was self-taught and had a natural sense of dramatic composition. He had a deep love of the West, and he was a working cowboy for 30 years during the great era of cowboy life. He was a trail driver, a ranch hand, a hunter, and a trapper. He also lived with native Indians and came to appreciate their way of life. His understanding of both true cowboy and Indian ways gave his paintings a deeply authentic, realistic, and sympathetic quality. His great fame came later in his life. While his first commission was from a saloon owner for a picture to hang behind the saloon bar, he later found fame with magazine illustrations and international exhibitions. His greatest honor, however, was the recognition and acceptance real working cowboys gave his art.

Charles Siringo

(1855–1928) Charles Siringo was one of the first working cowboys to successfully write about his experiences. His book *A Texas Cowboy: Or, 15 Years on the Hurricane Deck of a Spanish Pony* told of his exploits and adventures as a trail-driving cowboy. Will Rogers later said that Siringo's book was his inspiration to be a cowboy.

Belle Starr

(1848–1889) Belle Starr was one of the Wild West's most infamous women, deserving the name of the "Bandit Queen." She gained notoriety because of her participation in robberies, horse stealing, and a life of frontier crime. She traveled with many of the West's worst outlaws, including the James brothers and the Cole Younger gang. She was one of the wildest women in the West and came to a bad end herself. In 1889, a never-identified assailant shot her in the back and killed her.

John B. Stetson

(1830–1906) John B. Stetson played an important role in the American West by designing and developing the cowboy hat. The Stetson hat became identified with the image of the cowboy and became one of the cowboy's most useful work tools. Stetson came from a family of hatters, and he originally traveled to the West for health reasons. He noticed the various hats cowboys were wearing and in 1865 began production on the hat that would define the cowboy look for all time. Stetson hats became legendary for their quality and durability. His first cowboy hat was called the "Boss of the Plains" and was an enormous success. By the time of his death, his company was selling two million hats a year worldwide, and his name had become synonymous with cowboy hats.

William "Buck" Taylor

(1857–1924) "Buck" Taylor, star of the Wild West Shows, was the first really "glamorous" cowboy. He was billed as the "King of the Cowboys" in Buffalo Bill's Wild West Show, and he performed in numerous horse-back-riding acts. He was orphaned at a young age and worked as a cowboy to support himself. Taylor had worked for Bill Cody at the showman's Nebraska ranch before he joined the show. On February 1, 1887, a dime novel by Col. Prentiss Ingraham introduced "Buck Taylor, King of the Cowboys." With the publication of this pulp novel, William Taylor became America's first cowboy hero.

William "Buck" Taylor.

"80 John" Wallace

(1868–1939) Daniel Webster "80 John" Wallace was one of the first African-American ranchers in Texas. The son of slaves, he earned his nickname through his work as a cowboy and wrangler, branding a large "80" on cattle sides while he worked for a Texas cattleman, Clay Mann. Clay Mann later arranged a deal with Wallace in which part of Wallace's wages were invested for him to purchase his own herd. From this humble beginning, Wallace became a millionaire cattleman himself.

■ Was there really a cowboy code of honor?

Yes, there was a cowboy code of honor. For the most part, cowboys were honest, hard-working men who valued personal honor above all else. It was a time where a handshake could seal a deal, and a man's word was as good as gold. Movies have created the exaggerated impression that a personal slight would invariably result in a blazing gun battle. Closer to the truth is the idea that cowboys tried to lead honorable lives based upon a few simple precepts. Of course, major violations like murder, cattle rustling, or horse stealing were dealt with quickly and justly according to the "Code of the West." Most often though, a cowboy who did not live by the code of honor became a social outcast.

Of course, there was no written "Code of the West" available for cowboys to consult and use as guidance. Like many aspects of cowboy life, the code of honor was more a way of life passed down from generation to generation, an unspoken folk knowledge, that cowboys learned by listening and paying close attention to the ways and manners of other honorable cowboys.

Historians and writers have gathered lists of the code of honor as described by various cowboys who could articulate their own personal code of honor. Also, several famous cowboy figures have deliberately written their own lists to reflect their understanding of the cowboy code of honor. All these lists help us understand that the cowboy code of honor was really built around a single direct idea: Be an honest and reliable person in all your dealings.

Traditional folklore does contain many guidelines to what could be considered a cowboy code of honor. While no cowboy from the traditional era of the trail drives could probably recite the code, without a doubt he lived his life guided by it. Although there are many more, the following points of the cowboy code of conduct are examples of the way a cowboy tried to live his life.

The Cowboy Code of Conduct

No whisky with the wagon. No drinking was allowed on the trail drive.

Wake a man by speech, not touch. A man startled in his sleep might come up with his gun in his hand.

When riding up to a ranch or homestead, a cowboy shouts out "Hello the house" to make his presence known. He will stay on his horse until invited to dismount.

When two men meet on the trail, speak, and pass on, neither looks back. To look back means one rider does not trust the other rider.

Never wave to another rider on the trail. It might spook the horse.

When a cowboy sees a stranger on the trail, he rides straight toward him and greets him. Veering off the trail looks suspicious.

When approaching another rider from behind, give a shout.

A cowboy does not bother another man's horse.

A cowboy asks before borrowing another man's horse.

A cowboy has courage.

A cowboy keeps his word.

A cowboy never talks down to anyone. If one man dismounts, the other does too.

A cowboy is respectful to women.

A cowboy takes his place on the trail drive and ends the day in the same place.

A cowboy offers friendship to strangers.

A cowboy shares his grub with strangers.

A cowboy does not complain.

A cowboy is loyal.

A cowboy will risk his life to save his partner.

A cowboy never asks another cowboy about his past.

A cowboy does not cut in front of another rider on the trail.

A cowboy unbuckles his gun belt and removes his spurs before entering another's house.

A cowboy renders assistance whenever he is asked.

A cowboy settles his horse before he sits down to dinner.

A cowboy never talks rudely in front of a woman and always tips his hat.

Movie and Television Cowboy Codes of Conduct

Many movie and television shows developed their own codes of conduct based on the traditional cowboy code of conduct. These codes were often part of a membership card children received when they signed up for the show's cowboy club. By joining the club, the young cowboys pledged to honor the show's cowboy code.

Gene Autry's Cowboy Code

Singing and movie legend Gene Autry developed the following cowboy code. Gene Autry made more than 90 cowboy films and is acknowledged as the first genuine singing cowboy of the screen. His weekly radio show, *Gene Autry's Melody Ranch*, aired steadily for 16 years. He also was the first western star to film shows for television.

1.   A cowboy must never shoot first, hit a smaller man, or take unfair advantage.

2.   He must never go back on his word, or a trust confided in him.

3.   He must always tell the truth.

4.   He must be gentle with children, the elderly, and animals.

5.   He must not advocate or possess racially or religious intolerant ideas.

6.   He must help people in distress.

7.   He must be a good worker.

8.   He must keep himself clean in thought, speech, action, and personal habits.

9.   He must respect women, parents, and his nation's laws.

10.   The cowboy is a patriot.

Hopalong Cassidy's Creed for American Boys and Girls

Movie cowboy Hopalong Cassidy developed his Creed for American Boys and Girls. Hopalong Cassidy starred in more than 65 Hopalong films as well as a popular cowboy televison show in the 1950s.

1.   The highest badge of honor a person can wear is honesty. Be mindful at all times.

2.   Your parents are the best friends you have. Listen to them and obey their instructions.

3. If you want to be respected, you must respect others. Show good manners in every way.

4. Only through hard work and study can you succeed. Don't be lazy.

5. Your good deeds always come to light. So don't boast or be a show off.

6. If you waste your time or money today, you will regret it tomorrow. Practice thrift in all ways.

7. Many animals are good and loyal companions. Be friendly and kind to them.

8. A strong, healthy body is a precious gift. Be neat and clean.

9. Our country's laws are made for your protection. Observe them carefully.

10. Children in many foreign lands are less fortunate than you. Be glad and proud you are an American.

Roy Rogers's Riders Club Rules

Cowboy legend Roy Rogers and his Roy Rogers's Riders Club had their own cowboy code of conduct. Roy Rogers was known as the "King of the Cowboys." He starred in more than 100 movies as well as in popular radio and television shows.

1. Be neat and clean.

2. Be courteous and polite.

3. Always obey your parents.

4. Protect the weak and help them.

5. Be brave, but never take chances.

6. Study hard and learn all you can.

7. Be kind to animals and care for them.

8. Eat all your food and never waste any.

9. Love God and go to Sunday School regularly.

10. Always respect our flag and country.

■ When did all this cowboy stuff really happen?

A complete, detailed timeline of the origins and development of cowboy culture in the United States would fill a book by itself. Following is an abbreviated timeline of major events in cowboy history. It lists many of the major events that were important in the development of cowboy history and contributed to the modern cowboy myth.

11th century Spanish ranching originates on the Spanish peninsula.

1493 On his second voyage to the New World, Columbus brings the hardy Andalusian "black cattle" to the Caribbean Island he called Española, today the Dominican Republic and Haiti. This was the introduction of cattle and Spanish ranching practices to the New World.

1519 Hernán Cortés arrives in Mexico and brings 16 Andalusian horses (11 stallions and 5 mares), thereby reintroducing the horse to the New World.

1521 Gregorio de Villalobos transports calves from the Caribbean islands to mainland Mexico, the first cows on the mainland New World continent.

1550 The Spanish in the New World begin regular roundups of free-range cattle. The Spanish called these roundups *rodeos*, Spanish for to round up or gather.

1598 Spanish settlers, led by Juan de Oñate, move north, establishing ranches and introducing cattle to the El Paso area and north of the Rio Grande.

1600s Cattle graze and multiply north of the Rio Grande.

Early 1700s *Vaqueros* migrate from Mexico with Spanish missionaries to California and Texas.

1721 Marqués de Aguayo opens the south Texas cattle industry.

1748 José de Escandón develops the cradle of the western cattle industry by establishing *ranchos* in the huge expanse of land called the Nueces Strip, from the Rio Grande to the Nueces River.

1765   The French-Indian Wars end, opening the West for expansion and settlement by Americans living in the East. Many of these settlers will migrate to southern Texas, introducing them to Spanish/Mexican *vaquero* cowboy practices.

1767   Father Gaspar Jose de Solis inspects Texas missions and records "many Spanish cattle, unbranded and ownerless."

1769   Franciscan monk Junípero Serra begins establishing missions from San Diego to San Francisco. Native Indians working on the missions become California's first *vaqueros*. The first horses and cattle come to California.

Late 1700s–
Early 1800s   *Vaqueros* drive cattle from east Texas to Louisiana and Mexico.

Early 1800s   Anglos begin to arrive in what will become Texas and find Spanish/Mexican ranching traditions well established. Texas *vaqueros* teach the Anglo settlers the skills and craft of handling horses and cattle on the open range.

1815   The Conestoga wagon (prairie schooner, or covered wagon) becomes the favorite mode of transportation for settlers moving to the West. This wagon will become an icon of the West and a version of it will later be adapted for the chuck wagon during the great trail drives.

1821   Mexico declares its independence from Spain.

1820s–1830s   Slaves and freemen learn horse and cattle skills from the *vaqueros*—roping, riding, and branding.

1833   Samuel Colt invents the revolver. This gun became a legend in the West. While most real working cowboys seldom wore guns, no movie cowboy would be caught without a six-shooter strapped to his leg.

1836   The first successful revolver cartridge, a self-contained unit of primer, powder, and bullet, is invented.

1843   Jesse Chisholm starts an early trail drive, supplying cattle to Ft. Scott, Kansas, following a military road on the Missouri-Kansas border.

1844   Samuel Maverick, a farmer in Texas, accepts cattle in payment for a debt. Later, in 1856, he sells these cattle to A. Toutant Beauregard. Because Maverick had not branded these cattle, Beauregard's men sent to gather up these unbranded cattle call them "Mavericks." This is the origin of the word *maverick*, meaning loose, unbranded cattle.

1847   Roping and throwing contest held in Santa Fe, New Mexico, an early event in establishing the rodeo as a showcase of cowboy skills.

1848   Mexico loses over half its northern frontier to the United States. This land becomes the states of Texas, New Mexico, Arizona, Nevada, Utah, Colorado, and California. Mexican *vaqueros* continue to work in their new country, the United States.

1848   Gold is discovered at Sutter's Mill in California. The gold rush accelerates western migration.

1852   Henry Wells and William Fargo establish a company to provide horseback and stagecoach express delivery from the East to California. The Wells-Fargo Express becomes one of the legends of western lore.

1860   The cowboy boot begins to appear in its modern form.

        The Pony Express begins mail delivery between St. Joseph, Missouri, and Sacramento, California.

1865   John B. Stetson begins making a wide-brimmed felt hat that would become the cowboy hat of the West.

1866   Charles Goodnight designs the chuck wagon.

1867–1887   The primary era of the great cattle drives. Anglo cowboys use the cattle practices learned from the *vaqueros* to drive hundreds of thousands of cattle across great distances. *Vaqueros*, along with Black cowboys, make up approximately one-third of the cowboys working the cattle drives. During this period, American cowboy culture developed based upon the centuries-old skills and practices of the Spanish/Mexican *vaqueros*.

1869   The transcontinental railroad is completed at Promontory Point, Utah. Railroad access to eastern markets enhances the profits to be made from the great trail drives.

1873   Joseph F. Glidden invents and patents barbed wire. This wire, known as "the Devil's rope," allows farmers and ranchers to close off open range land and contributed to the end of the great trail drives.

Colt introduces its single-action revolver, the Peacemaker.

Winchester introduces its rifle and carbine.

Levi Strauss patents his copper-riveted pants.

1880   Charles Hyer opens a boot-making shop in Olathe, Kansas. Hyer boots become the boot of choice for working cowboys.

1886–1887   Severe winter storms kill the majority of range cattle, decimating the trail herds.

1887   The era of the great cattle drives comes to an end.

1880s   William Cody produces the Wild West Shows, beginning the myth of the American cowboy. *Vaqueros* perform in the shows, amazing audiences with their roping and riding skills. Chief Sitting Bull and Annie Oakley star in the shows. The shows bring the cowboy lore of the West to worldwide audiences.

1897   The first Frontier Day celebration is held in Cheyenne, Wyoming. Western celebrations such as this helped establish the rodeo and lore of the cowboy for public entertainment.

1903   The first western cowboy movie with a plot, *The Great Train Robbery*, is released. The movie introduces the first cowboy star actor, Max Anderson, known as Bronco Billy.

Bill Pickett invents bulldogging on a ranch in Texas.

1912   The Zane Grey novel *Riders of the Purple Sage* is published. This novel, along with more than 50 others, brings the myth of the cowboy to an even larger American public.

1929   The Cisco Kid movie *In Old Arizona* earns Warner Baxter the first Academy Award for a western actor.

1930   An epic western film, *The Big Trail*, directed by Raoul Walsh, stars an unknown actor named John Wayne.

1933   The Lone Ranger radio series debuts.

1933–1941   An estimated 1,230 western films are released.

1935   Hopalong Cassidy and Gene Autry begin their western film careers.

1938   Red Ryder comic strip character debuts.

1939   John Wayne stars in *Stagecoach*.

1940   The Gene Autry Melody Ranch radio show debuts on CBS radio.

1949   The Lone Ranger television series debuts.

1950   The Cisco Kid television series debuts.

1951   The Roy Rogers television series debuts.

1953   The Annie Oakley television series debuts, starring Gail Davis in the first TV series with a female lead role.

1958   A total of 31 westerns are offered in television prime time.

1959   The Rodeo Cowboy's Association holds its first National Finals Rodeo in Dallas.

1961   Country Music Hall of Fame opens.

1965   National Cowboy Hall of Fame opens in Oklahoma City.

■ What are the different contests in a rodeo?

The modern rodeo developed from the *vaquero* games and contests played during their cattle hunts. The Spanish word for the cattle hunts was *rodeo*, which meant to round up or surround. During these rodeos, the Spanish and Mexican *vaqueros* created entertaining contests to show off their cowboy skills.

The Anglo cowboys witnessed the *vaquero* contests and developed their own versions of the contests. They adopted the Spanish word *rodeo* and used it to name their own cowboy contests.

The historians of the Prescott Arizona Rodeo claim that the word *rodeo* was not commonly used for rodeo contests until the 1920s. Before 1920, people called the cowboy contests tournaments, fiestas, cowboy contests, and stampedes. By the 1930s, however, the word *rodeo* was commonly used to describe cowboy contests.

The modern rodeo first appeared in the late 1800s. It quickly became a successful substitute for the trail-drive experience for all of the out-of-work trail-drive cowboys. By the early 1900s, the rodeo was established as both a contest of cowboy skills and a western entertainment experience.

Women and men competed together in the early rodeos. Many women became rodeo stars and champions. The books by Judy Crandall, Mary LeCompte, and Joyce Gibson Roach listed in the Suggested Reading section at the end of this book are good reference books about the role of women in both the early and modern rodeo.

During the 1930s and 1940s, however, the rodeo began to evolve into its present form. Today, the rodeo contests are for men; women compete only in barrel racing.

Modern rodeo contests are divided into two categories: (1) those scored by a judge, and (2) those timed for speed. The contests scored by a judge are bareback bronc riding, saddle bronc riding, and bull riding. Those scored for speed are barrel racing, steer wrestling, and the roping contests.

Bareback bronc riding involves staying on a bucking horse for eight seconds. Two judges score the eight-second ride, scoring both the horse and rider on a 1–25-point scale. A perfect ride is 100 points. The judges score the horse for the quality of its bucking, and they score the rider on the quality of his riding and spurring. A bareback rigging, made of leather and rawhide and roughly resembling a suitcase handle, is the cowboy's grip during the ride. The cowboy must have one hand in the air throughout the ride. He is disqualified if he touches himself, the horse, or the equipment during the ride. The contest also involves a Spur Out Rule: the rider's spurs must be in contact with the horse, above the "break" of the shoulder, when the horse's front feet first touch the ground outside the chute.

Bareback bronc rider.

Saddle-bronc riding is the same one-handed, eight-second ride as bareback bronc riding, except that the cowboy uses a saddle. The scoring is the same as bareback riding. The contest also requires the cowboy to spur, and a cowboy who is not spurring out of the chute is disqualified. A rider also suffers disqualification if he touches the horse, himself, or his equipment with his free hand, if either foot slips out of a stirrup, or if he drops the rein.

Bull riding has become one of the most popular rodeo contests. It also is an eight-second ride, with two judges scoring both the rider and the bull, 25 points each, for a 100-point perfect score. Spurring is not required, but good spurring can add to a rider's score. The rider's body position—he must remain over the middle of the bull without tilting or leaning back—is an important factor in the score. The rider is disqualified if he touches himself, the bull, or the equipment.

Barrel racing is a women's contest and is a pure speed race. Riders race in a cloverleaf pattern around three barrels set in a triangle. The races are so fast, and the results are so close, that modern rodeos use electronic timers. Riders can touch or move a barrel, but they receive a five-second penalty if they knock it over. The rider with the quickest time is the winner.

Steer wrestling is a contest in which a rider leaps off his horse and captures a running steer by the head and horns. He then digs his heels into the ground and wrestles the steer to the ground. The cowboy must either wrestle the steer to the ground or change the direction of its body. The cowboy receives a 10-second penalty if he does not allow the steer a 10-second head start. A cowboy who crosses a rope barrier before the steer's 10-second head start receives the penalty. The cowboy with the quickest time wrestling the steer to the ground is the winner.

Rodeos have two roping events: (1) team roping, and (2) calf roping. The team roping involves two cowboys who compete as a team to rope a steer. One ropes the head and the other ropes the feet. The head roper must get the rope around both the steer's horns. The foot roper must get the rope around the feet. The judges stop the timer when the steer is stopped and roped and both ropes are pulled tight. Teams suffer a ten-second penalty if they "break the barrier" before the steer gets a 10-second head start. The team with the quickest time is the winner.

Calf roping involves chasing down a running calf, roping it, throwing it to the ground, and tying any three of its legs together. The cowboy uses a "pigging string" he has carried in his teeth to tie the calf's legs. The cowboy is disqualified if the calf's legs become loose within six seconds of the tie. As in other speed contests, the cowboy must not "break the barrier" before the calf gets a head start. The cowboy throws his arms into the air to signal the judges when he is through tying the calf's legs. The cowboy with the quickest time is the winner.

■ Were there any other cowboys besides the Mexican *vaqueros* and the American cowboy?

Yes, cowboys worked throughout the Americas tending to their horses and cattle. While the emphasis of this book is on the Mexican *vaquero* and the American cowboy, especially during the era of the great trail drives, the complete cowboy story in the Western Hemisphere includes cowboys from Canada to Chile.

All open-range cowboys of the Americas, including both North and South America, shared many important traits, including:

1. Their cattle and horses originated with and descended from the original cattle and horses the Spanish brought to the New World.

2. Their language, clothes, and tools of the trade derived from Spanish cattle culture.

3. Their knowledge of how to work with horses and cattle was based upon Spanish horse and cattle open-range practices.

4. Their work involved intense labor with horses and cattle.

5. No matter where they were, their work was remarkably similar: capturing, breaking, and training wild horses; rounding up and branding cattle; driving cattle to markets; and tending to both horses and cattle on open ranges.

6. Their golden era was in the 1800s.

7. They were poor rural workers who owned neither the animals they worked with nor the land they worked on.

8. They had a fierce and independent spirit.

In Canada, ranch culture flourished in its western provinces and prairies. Alberta, Canada, developed an especially strong ranch culture in the 1880s. The first Canadian roundup occurred in 1879. Throughout the 1800s, a cattle and ranching boom in Alberta created a demand for cowboys. Canadian cowboys were a mix of Canadian, British, and American cowboys.

In Colombia and Venezuela, the cowboy was called a *llanero*. Since the *llanos*, the open plains of Colombia and Venezuela, flooded annually from April to September, *llaneros* had to be adept swimmers and boatmen. Usually, cowboys could not swim at all and that is partially what made driving cattle across rivers so dangerous for cowboys.

In Argentina, the *gaucho* was the proud cowboy of the Argentinean ranges, the *pampas*. The *gaucho* worked cattle in the Río de la Plata, an area that today includes Argentina, Uruguay, Paraguay, and southern Brazil. *Gauchos* used *bolas*, balls or stones covered with rawhide and attached to long ropes, to capture animals. The *gauchos* swung the *bolas* over their heads and threw them at the animal's legs to capture them.

In Brazil, cowboys were called *vaqueiros* and *gaúchos*. Their names are similar to the Spanish names of other South American cowboys, but slightly different because the Brazilian people speak Portuguese instead of Spanish.

In Chile, the *huaso* was the hard-working cowboy of Chile's Central Valley plains. Like cowboys everywhere, the *huaso* was a strong worker who lived a simple and hard life working with horses and cattle

In Hawaii, the cowboy was called a *paniolo*. The Hawaiians imported horses and cattle to their islands in the late 1700s and early 1800s, but had no knowledge or skills of how to work with them. In 1832, Hawaii's King Kamehameha III imported Mexican *vaqueros* to the Hawaiian Islands to teach the natives ranch skills. The word *paniolo* was a corruption of the word *español*, the Spanish word for Spanish.

Richard Slatta's book, *Cowboys of the Americas*, is the best book for further information on cowboys of the Western Hemisphere.

Happy Trails to You

Places to Go and Things to Do to Learn More About Cowboys

■ How can I use the Internet to learn more about cowboys?

The Internet has a vast amount of sites about cowboys. There is no way a student could search them all. A simple Web search of the word *cowboy* on the Web search engine Google gave over one million sites! So, to cut that search down a little bit, here are some good sites to start your search. Many of these sites have links to other information sites and are good beginning guides for your research on cowboys.

All sites were accessed May 2002.

Cowboy History

http://www.AmericanWest.com/
A good site for links to other sites about the history and development of the American West.

http://www.wildwestweb.net/
Lots of good information about cowboy history. Links to other information sites.

http://www.pbs.org/weta/thewest/
Very informative site based upon a Ken Burns documentary series on the West, which premiered on PBS stations in September 1996. This multimedia guided tour proceeds chapter-by-chapter through each episode in the series, offering selected documentary materials, archival images, and commentary, as well as links to background information and other resources of the Web site.

http://www.oldwest.org/cows/links.html
Web site for the Old West Living History Foundation. Dozens of links to very informative Web sites. Lots of good information with a special section on cowboy and historical re-enactment specialists.

http://www.unm.edu/~gabbriel/index.html
Excellent site with informative details on cowboy history, especially that of the Spanish/Mexican *vaquero*.

http://members.aol.com/cmurphy93/Cowboys2/Contents.html
A site filled with links about cowboy life, history, and culture.

http://social.chass.ncsu.edu/slatta/index.htm
Home page of Richard Slatta, The Cowboy Professor. He has written several excellent books about cowboys and the West.

http://www.barbwiremuseum.com/cattlebrandhistory.htm
Informative site on barbed wire and cattle brands.

http://www.cowgirls.com
   Good site on western cowgirls. Dedicated to keeping the spirit of the early pioneer cowgirl alive.

http://www.net.westhost.com/trail1.htm
   Information about the great trail drives.

Cowboys of Color

http://www.coax.net/people/lwf/western.htm
   A good site with many links to information about people of color on America's western frontier.

http://www.mindstation.com/history/cowboy.html
   A biographical listing of Black pioneers, settlers, and cowboys.

http://www.blackcowboys.com
   Self-described as "The Premiere Black Cowboys Site on the Internet."

Cowboy Music and Movies

http://www.westernmusic.org/
   Western Music Association. Yup, it's all about cowboy music.

http://www.cowboypal.com/
   A great site about cowboy movies and movie legends.

http://www.vintagecowboymusic.com/
   A site with more than 1,000 audio and 1,500 video cowboy tapes for sale.

Cowboy Museums

http://www.royrogers.com/museum.html
   Fun site for the Roy Rogers–Dale Evans Museum.

http://www.oldwestmuseum.org
   Welcome to the Cheyenne Frontier Days™ Old West Museum where the vitality, drama, and romance of life in the West comes alive.

http://www.cowboyhalloffame.org
> The site for the National Cowboy and Western Heritage Museum. The Cowboy Hall of Fame is located at this site.

http://www.cowgirl.net/
> The site for the National Cowgirl Museum and Hall of Fame.

Cowboy Posters

http://www.vintageposters.com/
> Great place to look for cowboy movie posters.

Cowboy Poetry

http://www.westfolk.org/p.home.html
> Web site for the Western Folklife Center and the National Cowboy Poetry Gathering.

http://www.cowboypoetry.com/
> All about cowboy poetry.

Cowboy Miscellaneous Sites

http://www.prorodeo.com
> The site for the Professional Rodeo Cowboys Association. If you like the rodeo, this is the site for you.

http://www.mark-allen.com/
> A great site for western supplies, performing equipment, and videos.

http://www.wWAC.com/
> If you want to know about trick and fancy roping, gun-spinning, knife-throwing, whip-cracking, tomahawk throwing, trick riding and trick horses, this is the site for you.

http://www.cowboy.net/cowboy/index.html
   A site with many links on cowboy rodeo, literature, western gear, art, museums, and other cool cowboy sites.

http://www.cow-boy.com/index.htm
   Fun site geared for kids on cowboy life, lore, and legend. Join the Cowboy Heritage Club.

http://cyberrodeo.com/guysgals/index.html
   Howdy pardner! Welcome to Cowboys and Cowgirls, one of the best darn collections of western links on the Internet. Many interesting cowboy links.

■ What are some good cowboy movies?

Movies are the greatest entertainment invention of the twentieth century. Hollywood, through its movie- and celebrity-making machinery, is primarily responsible for creating the myth of the American cowboy. Through movies, the world has learned about the American cowboy. Hollywood not only has produced literally thousands of western-themed movies, it has also created a legion of movie stars who were famous for their cowboy characters.

The first question is what makes a really good cowboy movie? The easy answer, of course, is that a really good cowboy movie is one that you enjoy; but besides simply entertaining you, a good cowboy movie should also teach you something truthful about cowboys and their world.

The best movies are greatly entertaining, populated with engaging characters, and emotionally memorable. They also accurately portray the world in which the characters live so the audience members have a better understanding of the life and times of the characters in the movie. Although movies are not intended to be history lessons, the best ones are great history teachers.

The following list is intended to be an all-time cowboy classics list. Of course, publishing such a list is guaranteed to raise disagreement, because all lists are personal and subjective. Nevertheless, the movies on this list are the ones that most frequently appear on all-time best cowboy movie lists. They are well recognized for being very entertaining movies, but they are also respected for the accurate portrayal they give of the cowboy and his life and times.

Eight of the listed movies are on the American Film Institute 100 Greatest Movies List. Five are on the Recommended List for the American Film Institute 100 Greatest Movies List. Many are Oscar® Award winners. Film critics consider them all timeless classics. So, if you want to use the movies to teach you something more about cowboys and their world, these movies are a good place to start. The list is intended to be a guide to movies that are considered classics by most film experts. So pick up one, or a few, and enjoy learning more about cowboys by watching a good movie.

The Top Thirteen!

(The movies are listed in placement order on the American Film Institute 100 Greatest Movies List.) (Usually these lists are top ten lists, but there were too many good cowboy movies to limit the list to just ten selections.)

1. **The Treasure of Sierra Madre** (1948): No. 30 on the American Film Institute 100 Greatest Movies List. A classic about the search for gold in the Sierra Madre mountains, it tells the harsh story of the evil effects of greed and gold on men's souls. Directed by John Huston, it starred Humphrey Bogart and Walter Huston. The film won three Academy Award Oscars® for best supporting actor, best director, and best screenplay.

2. **High Noon** (1952): No. 33 on the American Film Institute 100 Greatest Movies List. A tense western thriller about a lone sheriff who is abandoned by his townspeople and single-handedly defeats a gang of desperadoes terrorizing the town. The film won four Oscars®, including best actor for Gary Cooper.

3. **Butch Cassidy and the Sundance Kid** (1969): No. 50 on the American Film Institute 100 Greatest Movies List. An entertaining comedy/ drama starring Paul Newman and Robert Redford, the story features the friendship and camaraderie between two legendary outlaws. Instead of the usual violent gun battles of most western films, this movie entertained with its story of the endearing exploits and light, bantering dialogue of its two outlaw heroes. The film is atypical from the usual western because of its humor and light-hearted action. Nominated for seven Oscars®, it won four.

4. **Stagecoach** (1939): No. 63 on the American Film Institute 100 Greatest Movies List. Directed by John Ford and starring John Wayne, *Stagecoach* is set in majestic Monument Valley. Film critics consider it a landmark film because it elevated the western movie from Saturday matinee "B" movie status to serious drama. The story is one of tight tension as nine stagecoach passengers are tested and challenged on a dangerous journey through Monument Valley. The film was nominated for seven Oscars® and won two.

5. **Shane** (1953): No. 69 on the American Film Institute 100 Greatest Movies List. Starring Alan Ladd in his best-known role, *Shane* was the most successful western of the 1950s. The movie has everything: Technicolor, the battle between good and evil, the settling of the western frontier, lawless desperadoes, an innocent boy, and a gun-slinging hero trying to escape his violent past. Nominated for six Oscars®, it won one.

6. **The Wild Bunch** (1969): No. 80 on the American Film Institute 100 Greatest Movies List. Directed by Sam Pechinpah, *The Wild Bunch* is controversial because it graphically depicts violence in telling its story of the dying West. The film tells the story of an aging bunch of outlaws who discover that the code of the West has changed, and they are no longer able to survive in the new frontier era. Film critics hail its extremely realistic vision of the last days of a dying breed—the outlaw desperado. The film was nominated for two Oscars®. ·

7. **The Searchers** (1956): No. 96 on the American Film Institute 100 Greatest Movies List. Another great classic western film directed by John Ford, set in Monument Valley, and starring John Wayne. The film tells the gripping story of a loner, driven by hate and revenge, who searches for his two nieces who have been stolen by Indians. John Wayne considered this his favorite role.

8. **Unforgiven** (1992): No. 98 on the American Film Institute 100 Greatest Movies List. Film icon Clint Eastwood produced, directed, and starred in this western classic. Eastwood plays a retired gunslinger who takes one last job to avenge the brutal disfigurement of a dance hall lady and to claim the reward for killing the man who assaulted her. The film is a dark portrayal of the cruel realities of western violence. It deftly debunks the romanticized myth of the western gunslinger, and it brings a much-needed reality to the myth of the heroic gunfighter. A major commercial and critical success, the film was nominated for nine Oscars®, winning four, including the Oscar® for best picture and best director.

9. **My Darling Clementine** (1946): Recommended List for the American Film Institute 100 Greatest Movies List. Another western classic directed by John Ford, starring Henry Fonda and Victor Mature. The film tells the story of the famous shootout at the legendary OK Corral in Tombstone, Arizona, between Wyatt Earp, Doc Holliday, and the notorious Clanton gang.

10. **Red River** (1948): Recommended List for the American Film Institute 100 Greatest Movies List. Directed by Howard Hawkes and starring John Wayne and Montgomery Clift, *Red River* tells the epic story of a cattle drive historically based on the opening of the Chisholm Trail. The tough story pits two men, John Wayne and his adopted son, Montgomery Clift, as they bring a cattle herd to market on a brutal journey across the new Chisholm Trail. The film was nominated for two Oscars®

11. **Cat Ballou** (1965): Recommended List for the American Film Institute 100 Greatest Movies List. Starring Jane Fonda and Lee Marvin, *Cat Ballou* is a delightful western comedy that tells the story of a teacher in the Old West who joins with a gang of colorful outlaws to save the town from true outlaws. The movie had five Oscar® nominations, with Lee Marvin winning for best actor.

12. **Little Big Man** (1970): Recommended List for the American Film Institute 100 Greatest Movies List. Directed by Arthur Penn and starring Dustin Hoffman and Faye Dunaway. The film is an epic story of a man who lived through the taming of the West. Critics consider the film to be one of the best historical dramas about the settling of the West. Dustin Hoffman stars as Jack Crabb, a 121-year-old man who reminisces about all the famous events of the history of the West. Chief Dan George was nominated for an Oscar® for best supporting actor as Old Lodge Skins. The movie is one of the few westerns to sympathetically portray Native American history during the settlement of the West.

13. **Destry Rides Again** (1939): Recommended List for the American Film Institute 100 Greatest Movies List. Starring James Stewart and Marlene Dietrich in what critics consider a bit of inspired casting and image reversal, *Destry Rides Again* is a western comedy/spoof/farce. It parodies the classic western film elements: the lawless western town, the brave hero, and the dancehall woman with a heart of gold.

Other Recommended Movies

Although these movies did not make the top thirteen, they are all classics in their own right and worth viewing for the cowboy fan. Some were contenders for the American Film Institute 100 Greatest Movies List. They are available in video, and a sharp eye will often find these gems airing on late night television. There are no grade "B" cowboy movies on this list.

The Great Train Robbery (1903)

The Virginian (1929)

Cimarron (1931)

Viva Villa! (1934)

Annie Oakley (1935)

The Last of the Mohicans (1936)

Drums Along the Mohawk (1939)

Northwest Passage (1940)

The Ox-Bow Incident (1943)

Duel in the Sun (1946)

Fort Apache (1948)

She Wore a Yellow Ribbon (1949)

Gunfight at the OK Corral (1957)

3:10 to Yuma (1957)

Rio Bravo (1959)

The Magnificent Seven (1960)

The Man Who Shot Liberty Valance (1962)

Lonely Are the Brave (1962)

Ride the High Country (1962)

How the West Was Won (1963)

Shenandoah (1965)

Once Upon a Time in the West (1969)

True Grit (1969)

A Man Called Horse (1970)

McCabe and Mrs. Miller (1971)

The Outlaw Josey Wales (1976)

The Shootist (1976)

Young Guns (1988)

Lonesome Dove (1989) (television miniseries)

Dances with Wolves (1990)

■ What are some good vacation spots to learn more about cowboys?

There are many interesting vacation spots that feature western-themed family activities. The following listings are some of the most famous national vacation sites. The information listed under each heading is from the site's Web page information.

Autry Museum of Western Heritage
4700 Western Heritage Way
Los Angeles, CA 90027
323-667-2000
http://www.autry-museum.org
> The Autry Museum is devoted to preserving and interpreting the rich history and traditions of the American West. With one of the most comprehensive collections of western history and art, its seven permanent galleries and special exhibitions offer material gathered from the many cultures and events that have shaped the legacy of this vast region. The Autry Museum offers an entertaining and educational opportunity to discover the legacy of the American West.

Buffalo Bill Grave and Museum
987-1/2 Lookout Mountain Road
Golden, CO 80401
303-526-0747
http://www.buffalobill.org
> Buffalo Bill's Museum and Grave has many events throughout the year. One of the most popular is the re-enactment of his burial, complete with the ceremonial parade up the Lariat Loop Trail, the grieving bride, and Cavalry salute. Each year draws a larger audience to remember this great man.
> Visit the one and only grave of William F. "Buffalo Bill" Cody. By his request, Buffalo Bill was buried on Lookout Mountain in 1917, overlooking the Great Plains and the Rockies. Feel the breezes from the high peaks of the Continental Divide, smell the ponderosa pines, and watch the mountain wildlife, all just 30 minutes from downtown Denver.

Buffalo Bill Historical Center
720 Sheridan Avenue
Cody, WY 82414
307-587-4771
www.bbhc.org

The Buffalo Bill Historical Center is widely regarded as America's finest western museum. Located in northwestern Wyoming, 52 miles from Yellowstone National Park's east gate, the center features four internationally acclaimed museums under one roof.

Founded over 75 years ago as the Buffalo Bill Memorial Association, the center's four-museum complex consists of the Whitney Gallery of Western Art, the Buffalo Bill Museum, the Plains Indian Museum, and the Cody Firearms Museum. In addition to the four museums, the center also houses the Harold McCracken Research Library. The center is also in the midst of constructing the Draper Museum of Natural History.

Cheyenne Frontier Days™
Cheyenne Frontier Days Tickets
P.O. Box 2477
Cheyenne, WY 82003-2477
307-778-7222; 800-227-6336
http://www.cfdrodeo.com/

Cheyenne Frontier Days™ has become America's premier celebration of the West, but its roots are 100 percent pure high-octane rodeo. The first Frontier Days was held in 1897, long before the word *rodeo* was even used. Saddle-bronc riding was the featured event, although they called it "bucking and pitching" in those days.

Today, Cheyenne rodeo spectators are treated to more cowboy, bronc, bull, steer, and calf action every afternoon than they would likely see during the entire run of another rodeo—and it all takes place in the biggest rodeo arena in the West. The world's largest and most action-packed rodeo and many other events that take place during Cheyenne Frontier Days,™ the last full week of July, combine to make this celebration truly the "Daddy of 'em All."®

Gene Autry Oklahoma Museum
P.O. Box 67
Gene Autry, OK 73436
580-294-3047
http://www.cow-boy.com/museum.htm

The museum houses an outstanding collection of memorabilia from Gene Autry, Roy Rogers, Rex Allen, Tex Ritter, Jimmy Wakely, Eddie

Dean, and many others who appeared in the much-loved musical westerns of the 1930s and 1940s.

Museum of the Cariboo Chilcotin
113 North 4th Avenue
Williams Lake, BC V2G 2C8
Canada
250-392-7404
http://www.cowboy-museum.com/

A true cowboy museum. The Museum of the Cariboo Chilcotin is dedicated to preserving and promoting ranching heritage. It is the only museum in British Columbia to focus on ranching and rodeo, and it honors both the cowboys of the past and the present. The museum is home to the BC Cowboy Hall of Fame and a special display area features photos, biographies, and memorabilia of the province's outstanding cowboys. Rodeo and ranching go hand in hand, especially in Williams Lake, which is a major cattle-shipping center and hosts a number of rodeos each year. Rodeo displays are featured along with the ranching history. While the museum focuses on the history of ranching, the artistic side of cowboy culture is not forgotten. The museum features the work of western artists and holds a western art show each May. Recent renovations include a gallery designed to promote the work of painters and craftspeople. The gift store features western poets and musicians.

The National Cowboy Poetry Gathering
Western Folklife Center
501 Railroad St.
Elko, NV 89801
775-738-7508; 888-880-5885
http://www.westernfolklife.org/

The Western Folklife Center believes that cultural diversity contributes to the vitality and quality of American life and has committed itself to preserving, presenting, and perpetuating the varied traditions of the American West. Through research, documentation, public performances, media, exhibits, and educational programs, the Western Folklife Center honors the rich heritage and contemporary culture of the people of the West.

Every January, cattle people, rural folks, poets, musicians, gear makers, western enthusiasts, and urbanites tired of the teeming city gather in Elko, Nevada. From Saturday to Saturday, the town welcomes visitors to the Cowboy Poetry Gathering—a festival of conversation, singing, dancing, great hats and boots, stories, laughing and crying, big steaks, incessant rhymes, and a galloping cadence that keeps time for a solid week.

National Cowboy and Western Heritage Museum
1700 N.E. 63rd Street
Oklahoma City, OK 73111
(405) 478-2250
http://www.cowboyhalloffame.org

      The mission of the National Cowboy and Western Heritage Museum is to preserve and interpret the heritage of the American West for the enrichment of the public. Opened in 1965, the National Cowboy and Western Heritage Museum was originally conceived as a tribute to the men and women who helped establish the West as an integral part of America's cultural heritage.

      Visitors view art from Prix de West Award winners, the finest contemporary artists in the nation, as well as significant works by master artists Charles Russell, Frederic Remington, and Albert Bierstadt, among others. Visitors are awed by James Earle Fraser's famous 18-foot sculpture, End of the Trail; Colorado sculptor Gerald Balciar's 16,000-pound white marble cougar, aptly named Canyon Princess; and Windows to the West, five breathtaking western landscapes by Albuquerque artist Wilson Hurley.

      The sprawling complex also contains Prosperity Junction, a 14,000-square-foot, turn-of-the-century western town, and three major exhibition galleries: the American Cowboy Gallery, the American Rodeo Gallery, and the Western Entertainment Gallery. The Joe Grandee Museum of the Frontier West Gallery opened in April 2000, and in the fall of 2000, the Native American Gallery opened.

The National Cowgirl Museum and Hall of Fame
111 West 4th Street, Suite 300
Fort Worth, TX 76102
817-336-4475
http://www.cowgirl.net

      Beginning in the Texas panhandle town of Hereford in 1975, and now located in Fort Worth, the National Cowgirl Museum and Hall of Fame is the only museum in the world dedicated to honoring and documenting the lives of women who have distinguished themselves while exemplifying the spirit of the American West. These outstanding women include cowgirls and ranch women, writers, artists, teachers, and entertainers.

National Western Stock Show and Rodeo
National Western Complex
4655 Humboldt St.
Denver, CO 80216
303-297-1166 x810
www.nationalwestern.com

Approaching its 100th anniversary, the National Western Stock Show and Rodeo is one of America's best and largest rodeos and livestock and horse shows. It also features such special events as an extravagant Mexican rodeo and western exhibits. A great family event.

The Pro Rodeo Hall of Fame and Museum of the American Cowboy
101 Pro Rodeo Drive
Colorado Springs, CO 80919
719-528-4764
http://www.pikes-peak.com/rodeo

To some, rodeo is a sport. To others, it's a business. But to most competitors, rodeo is simply a way of life. Professional rodeo is the only major competitive sport that has evolved from a working lifestyle. Its development over the years is brought to life in the Pro Rodeo Hall of Fame and Museum of the American Cowboy.

This is the only museum in the world devoted exclusively to the sport of rodeo and the men and women who have made it a world-class sporting event. Visitors are treated to the Hall of Champions gallery, art exhibits, two video theatre presentations, rodeo and cowboy gear and memorabilia, live rodeo animals, a rodeo arena, a sculpture garden, and a unique Rodeo America store.

The Roy Rogers–Dale Evans Museum
15650 Seneca Road
Victorville, CA 92392
760-243-4547; 760-243-4548
http://www.royrogers.com/museum.html

The Roy Rogers–Dale Evans Museum serves as a recognizable landmark for those who travel the I-15 highway. Many who pass the frontier fortress with its larger-than-life Trigger are reminded of a couple who devoted their lives to making young and old happy by keeping the spirit of the American West alive. Housed inside the exhibit walls are memories and treasures of two lifetimes and all that they loved—a permanent reminder of a simple and innocent time when many Americans dreamed of living the exciting adventures of the "King of the Cowboys."

You'll find family photos dating back to Roy's and Dale's childhoods, colorful costumes, parade saddles, memorabilia from the silver screen and television, artifacts from Roy's real-life safari adventures, fan mail, comic strips, Roy's and Dale's Remington collection, tributes to Roy's friends and sidekicks, and much, much more!

Texas Cowboy Hall Of Fame
128 E. Exchange—Barn A
Fort Worth, TX
(817) 626-7131
http://www.texascowboyhalloffame.com/
The Texas Cowboy Hall of Fame is located in the Fort Worth Stockyards National Historic District. The museum features top cowboys and cowgirls such as Ty Murray, seven-time world champion all-around cowboy; Don Gray, eight-time World Champion Bullrider; and Charmayne James, ten-time world champion barrel racer. It also features the Sterquell Wagon Display, more than 60 antique wagons offering a view of the past—when the horse was king.

Wild West Arts Club National Convention
3945 W. Reno Avenue, Suite F
Las Vegas, NV 89118
800-858-5568
http://www.wWAC.com/
Are you interested in learning more about trick and fancy roping, whip cracking, gun spinning, fast draw, and all the other western arena arts? The national convention in Las Vegas features four days of lessons and seminars with professionals working alongside beginners and enthusiasts. You'll see showcase acts and contests, learn all you want, and have the time of your life.

Dude Ranches

Dude ranches are great fun vacations a family or an individual can take to learn about modern cowboys and the ways of the West. Almost every western state has dude ranches to visit, giving you the opportunity to ride horses and learn about the work of the modern ranch cowboy. They are usually hands-on experiences that are fun for all ages.

There are two kinds of dude ranches: (1) the guest ranch, and (2) the working ranch. Check carefully what type of ranch you sign up for so you get the type of ranch vacation you want.

At the guest ranch, the guest is truly a guest and is not expected to do any of the work on the ranch. Of course the guests can ride horses, but they can also have a leisurely ranch vacation filled with fishing, swimming, and hiking.

The second type, the working ranch, is for the vacationer who wants a working vacation and wants to be involved with whatever work is happening at the ranch. This can include a roundup, branding, and cattle drives. A working ranch will not be as fancy as a guest ranch, but it is as close as a city person can get to the cowboy life today.

To be fair and not give any dude ranch special favoritism, I have listed the following Internet sites as excellent starting places for finding a dude ranch near you. Good luck with your Internet search for the perfect dude ranch and vacation for your family!

America's Best Dude Ranches, Guest Ranches, and Vacation Farms
http://www.virtualcities.com/ons/dude.htm

Dude Ranches of North America
http://www.duderanches.com/

RANCHWEB 2001, the world's leading Internet site for dude ranches
http://www.ranchweb.com/

The Dude Ranchers' Association
http://www.duderanch.org/

Old West Dude Ranch Vacations
http://gorptravel.gorp.com/dude_search_main.asp

Suggested Readings

There are literally thousands of books written about cowboys. A person could go to the library and choose a book almost at random and still find a useful and helpful book. This short bibliography lists the major books consulted for this project. Each entry contains commentary on its merits as a reference. They are to assist the reader who is searching for direction and help in making decisions on where to start and which references to use for further and more in-depth research. They are also meant as guides for the reader interested in selecting books for more casual pleasure reading.

For starters, I recommend the books by Jo Mora, Will James, J. Frank Dobie, Arnold Rojas, and Edward Abbott. They are available through inter-library loan and all are excellent first-hand accounts of cowboy life. These books give the beginning scholar a good background in the personal history of cowboys before moving on to the more rigorous and detailed academic history books.

The books marked with a star, ★, are especially suited for young readers.

Abbott, Edward. *We Pointed Them North: Recollections of a Cowpuncher*. New York: Farrar & Rinehart, 1939.

Abbott's book is considered one of the best books ever written about the cowboy life written by a working cowboy.

Adams, Ramon F. *Cowboy Lingo: A Dictionary of the Slack-Jaw Words and Whangdoodle Ways of the American West*. New York: Houghton Mifflin, 2000.

A classic guide to the ways and words of cowboy life, this book is the only reference you will need to learn everything about the slang and distinctive language of the cowboy. Fun reading, too!

Axelrod, Alan, ed. *Ranching Traditions: Legacy of the American West*. New York: Abbeville Press, 1989.

A big and beautiful coffee-table book about modern ranching, containing essays by a dozen of the West's most distinguished western writers about all aspects of ranch life. Gorgeous photographs.

Baillargeon, Morgan, and Leslie Tepper, eds. *Legends of Our Times: Native Cowboy Life.* Vancouver: UBC Press, 1998.

An interesting book about the generally unknown life of Indian cowboys and their world of ranching and rodeo, covering the cowboy era from the turn of the last century to contemporary times. Contains historical and modern photography, as well as abundant information, including stories, art, and poetry on Indian culture and history with respect to cowboy life and ranching.

Brash, Sarah, ed. *Settling the West.* Alexandria, VA: Time-Life Books, 1996.

You will never go wrong with a Time-Life series book. An excellent and thorough history with very extensive photography and illustrations.

Cannon, Hal. *Cowboy Poetry: A Gathering.* Salt Lake City, UT: Gibbs M. Smith, 1985.

A small, but enjoyable book filled with modern cowboy poetry.

★ Cody, Tod. *The Cowboy's Handbook: How to Become a Hero of the Wild West.* New York: Cobblehill Books, 1996.

A brief, fun, children's book written by a descendent of William Cody (Buffalo Bill).

Crandall, Judy. *Cowgirls: Early Images and Collectibles.* Atglen, PA: Schiffer Publishing, 1994.

History told through the photographs of the time using wonderful and abundant historical photographs with descriptive notations. Features photography and biographies from the early days of rodeo when women competed with men and became rodeo champions. A small section on cowgirl collectibles is an additional bonus.

Cusic, Don. *Cowboys and the Wild West: An A–Z Guide from the Chisholm Trail to the Silver Screen.* New York: Facts on File, 1994.

An excellent encyclopedia and reference book on the West and cowboys, with easy-to-find information. Contains many photographs of cowboy movie stars.

Daniels, George D., ed. *The Spanish West.* Alexandria, VA: Time-Life Books, 1979.

The Time-Life books are always excellent references. This one covers the history and influence of the Spanish on the American West.

Dary, David. *Cowboy Culture: A Saga of Five Centuries.* Lawrence: University Press of Kansas, 1989.

This is one of the best reference books about cowboys and the development of cowboy culture in the West. Many of the other books quote this book. Containing excellent information about the Spanish and Mexican contributions to the history and development of the American cowboy, this is the only book you'll need for scholarly, in-depth information.

★ Dillman, Bruce. *The Cowboy Handbook: A Guide to Your Cowboy Heritage.* Kansas City: Lone Prairie Publishing, 1994.

"The CowBoy Handbook has something for everyone who values our cowboy heritage. Whether you're riding the range yourself or watching your favorite silver screen hero, this book makes a great sidekick!"—Gene Autry. Gene's already said it best. This is a good in-depth, but easy-reading, reference book on all things cowboy.

Dobie, J. Frank. *A Vaquero of the Brush Country.* Dallas: The Southwest Press, 1929.

J. Frank Dobie is one of the most respected western writers. This older book is considered one of the classics, a must read for the amateur scholar. An easy-to-read anecdotal approach to regional history.

Durham, Philip, and Everett L. Jones. *The Negro Cowboys.* Lincoln: University of Nebraska Press, 1983.

An historical examination of the role of the African-American cowboy.

★ Emrich, Duncan. *The Cowboy's Own Brand Book.* New York: Dover Publications, 1995.

A good beginner's guide to cattle brands.

Forbis, William H. *The Cowboys.* New York: Time-Life Books, 1973.

This is an excellent research book with very thorough information on all aspects of cowboy history and life and extensive historical photography. The Time-Life series is an excellent reference.

Freedman, Russell. *Cowboys of the Wild West.* New York: Clarion Books, 1985.

Historical accounts of cowboy life and work from an award-winning author. Includes excerpts from published cowboy recollections and contains abundant historical photographs.

★ ———. *In the Days of the Vaqueros, America's First True Cowboys.* New York: Clarion Books, 2001.

An excellent, easy-reading book about a seldom-covered aspect of cowboy history, the role of the *vaquero* in the history of the cowboy.

★ Gintzler, A. S. *Rough and Ready Cowboys.* Santa Fe, NM: John Muir Publications, 1994.

A good, brief introductory book about cowboys; simple, but informative.

★ Helberg, Kristin. *Cowboys: Color and Story Album.* Los Angeles: Troubador Press, 1982.

Another brief introductory book about cowboy life and work. The illustrations are black-and-white line drawings intended for coloring.

Jackman, Jack. *Los Mesteños: Spanish Ranching in Texas, 1721–1821.* College Station: Texas A&M University Press, 1986.

This is an excellent and scholarly book about the history of Spanish ranching in Texas. A very detailed and complete examination and highly recommended for the person seeking in-depth information on the importance of Spanish ranching.

James, Will. *All in the Day's Riding.* Missoula, MT: Mountain Press Publishing Company, 1998.

An excellent first-hand narrative account of his cowboy life by this famous author and illustrator. Great reading.

★ Kalman, Bobbie. *Bandannas, Chaps, and Ten-Gallon Hats.* New York: Crabtree Publishing, 1999.

A simple and brief book about various aspects of the cowboy world, with excellent color illustrations. An excellent reference for kids.

★ ———. *Life on the Trail.* New York: Crabtree Publishing, 1999.

Another excellent reference for kids.

Katz, William Loren. *The Black West: A Documentary and Pictorial History.* Garden City, NY: Doubleday, 1971.

This is a very thorough and detailed history of African-Americans and their role in settling the West; contains excellent archival photography.

LeCompte, Mary Lou. *Cowgirls of the Rodeo*. Urbana and Chicago: University of Illinois Press, 2000.

A very detailed book about the history of women's participation in the American rodeo; all the names, dates, and facts are here. Excellent scholarship at the service of little-known history.

★ Lester, Julius. *Black Cowboys, Wild Horses: A True Story*. New York: Dial Books, 1998.

The true story of Bob Lemmons, a former slave who became a cowboy. The book tells of his most famous adventure, in which he leads a herd of wild mustangs back to the corral. Containing wonderful watercolor illustrations of horses, this is a fun book for elementary school kids.

Lindmier, Tom, and Steve Mount. *I See by Your Outfit: Historic Cowboy Gear of the Northern Plains*. Glendo, WY: High Plains Press, 1996.

Illustrated descriptions and history of the clothes and tools of the cowboy's trade.

McCracken, Harold. *The American Cowboy*. Garden City, NY: Doubleday, 1973.

An easy-reading history book, containing full-color paintings and drawings by famous artists of the Old West.

McDowell, Bart. *The American Cowboy in Life and Legend*. Washington, DC: The National Geographic Society, 1972.

Containing first-hand accounts of cowboy life, this book covers cowboy history up through modern movie myths and Mexican *charros*. Excellent National Geographic–style color photography of cowboys and ranch people. Reads easily, almost like a novel.

Mora, Jo. *Californicos: The Saga of the Hard-Riding Vaqueros, America's First Cowboys*. Ketchum, ID: Dober Hill, Ltd., 1994.

Jo Mora is a legendary western writer/illustrator. This book is a very enjoyable account of Mora's experiences as a working *vaquero* and contains excellent illustrations. Highly recommended for the historical beginner.

———. *Trail Dust and Saddle Leather*. Lincoln: University of Nebraska Press, 1987.

More of Mora's excellent writing and illustrations. A great introductory book. An easy reading approach to history.

★ Morris, Michele. *Saddlebag Guide for Dudes, Tenderfeet and Cowpunchers Everywhere*. New York: Simon & Schuster, 1993.

An informative, well-illustrated book written with an insider's perspective. Ms. Morris grew up on the family cattle ranch.

★ Pelta, Kathy. *Cattle Trails: "Git Along Little Dogies . . ."* Austin: Raintree Steck-Vaughn, 1997.

This is a good, brief, general information book about cowboy life and work.

★ Pinkney, Andrea D. *Bill Pickett: Rodeo-Ridin' Cowboy*. San Diego: Harcourt, Brace & World, 1996.

An illustrated children's book about the famous African-American cowboy.

★ Potter, Edgar "Frosty." *Cowboy Slang: Colorful Cowboy Sayings*. Phoenix: Golden West Publishers Co., 1995.

More than 2,000 cowboy sayings organized by topic, with additional material on branding and the rodeo. Enjoyable, easy reading.

Roach, Joyce Gibson. *The Cowgirls*. Denton: University of North Texas Press, 1990.

"From ranches to Wild West show and rodeo; from dime novels and fiction to song, jokes, tall tales, and the movies; from the frontier to the footlights—that's what *The Cowgirls* is all about!" This is from the book cover and tells it just like it is. A very enjoyable and informative book.

Rojas, Arnold R. *Lore of the California Vaquero*. Fresno, CA: Academy Library Guild, 1958.

First-hand accounts by one of the last true *vaqueros*. Easy reading.

———. *Last of the Vaqueros*. Fresno, CA: Academy Library Guild, 1960.

Another excellent Rojas account of the last days of a working California cowboy.

Rollins, Philip A. *The Cowboy: An Unconventional History of Civilization on the Old-Time Cattle Range*. New York: Charles Scribner's Sons, 1936.

This is an older, but very complete and detailed reference book about all aspects of the cowboy world. It contains no pictures or illustrations, but the text is filled with interesting facts and information.

★ Ross, Stewart. *Cowboys: Fact or Fiction.* Brookfield, CT: Copper Beech Books, 1995.

A simple and brief, but informative, overview of cowboy history and life, with entertaining color illustrations.

Sandler, Martin W. *Cowboys: A Library of Congress Book.* New York: HarperCollins, 1994.

A detailed history book containing many excellent historical photographs from the Library of Congress.

Savage, Candace. *Cowgirls.* Berkeley, CA: Ten Speed Press, 1996.

Rich history and easy reading about the women of the West; this book covers everyone from Annie Oakley, to the rodeo circuit bronc busters, to the cowgirls of the Hollywood westerns. Wonderful historical photographs!

Seidman, Laurence I. *Once in the Saddle: The Cowboy Frontier, 1866–1896.* New York: Alfred A. Knopf, 1973.

Interesting eyewitness accounts to cowboy history. The illustrations are contemporary prints or photographs, maps, etchings, and political cartoons, plus many songs with music.

Slatta, Richard W. *Cowboys of the Americas.* New Haven, CT: Yale University Press, 1990.

This book has a much broader scope than most cowboy books; it covers both North and South American cowboys, and contains excellent first-hand descriptions of cowboy and ranch life.

———. *The Cowboy Encyclopedia.* Santa Barbara, CA: ABC-CLIO, 1994.

The title tells it all. A wonderful reference book loaded with information. More than 450 entries covering everything you would ever want to know about cowboys. Recommended as a best reference book by both *Library Journal* and the American Library Association.

★ Stewart, Gail B. *Cowboys in the Old West.* San Diego: Lucent Books, 1995.

Another good, brief, general information book about cowboy life and work with interesting black-and-white historical photography.

★ Stotter, Mike. *The Wild West*. New York: Kingfisher, 1997.

Excellent youth-oriented and informative book about the West. Puts cowboy life in the larger context of Native American tribal life and the settling of the American western frontier. Many color illustrations.

★ "The Old Wrangler." *How to Talk Cowboy: Sayings of the Old West*. Idaho Springs, CO: Saddle Sore Productions, 1999.

A fun book filled with all the clever sayings, wisdom, and humor of the cowboy world. A good beginning resource.

★ ———. *How to Walk Cowboy, or You Can Talk the Talk but Can You Walk the Walk*. Idaho Springs, CO: Saddle Sore Productions, 2000.

Another great little resource book from "The Old Wrangler." Filled with cowboy wisdom and humor.

Vigil, Arnold, ed. *Enduring Cowboys: Life in the New Mexico Saddle*. Santa Fe: New Mexico Magazine, 1999.

A wonderful coffee-table book about the modern New Mexico cowboy containing fascinating first-hand biographies of working ranch cowboys and cowgirls with accompanying photographs. The text covers cowboy history from the Spanish/Mexican era to the heyday of the Hollywood screen cowboy hero.

Ward, Fay E. *The Cowboy at Work: All About His Job and How He Does It*. New York: Hastings House, 1958.

A richly detailed book about the various aspects of the cowboy's daily work. All the illustrations and facts you will need. One of the best for detailed line drawings.

★ Zauner, Phyllis. *The Cowboy: An American Legend*. Sonoma, CA: Zanel Publications, 1994.

A good, easy-reading book about all things cowboy; has a good chapter about the beginnings of the movie cowboy. Also has some good quotes from cowboy experiences.

Zurhorst, Charles. *The First Cowboys and Those Who Followed*. New York: Abelard-Schuman, 1973.

Short biographical sketches of early cowboys, historical characters, and settlers of the West.

Permissions and Credits

Every effort has been made to trace the copyright holders. The publisher apologizes for any unintentional omissions and would be pleased, in such cases, to place an acknowledgment in future editions of this book.

Grateful acknowledgement is made to the following for permission to use photographs from their collections:

Buffalo Bill Historical Center, Charles J. Belden Collection:

> page 23, P.67.47, reprinted by permission.
>
> page 70, P.67.28, reprinted by permission.

Colorado Historical Society:

> page xx, negative number F-3538 10026767, reprinted by permission.
>
> page 44, top, negative number F-14800 10026001, reprinted by permission.
>
> page 44, bottom, negative number F-502 10026768, reprinted by permission.
>
> page 50, negative number J1467 20101467, William H. Jackson, reprinted by permission.
>
> page 54, negative number F-6321 10027812, reprinted by permission.
>
> page 62, negative number F-5581 10027814, reprinted by permission.
>
> page 63, negative number F-14983 10027813, reprinted by permission.
>
> page 74, negative number A58 20010058, Aultman, reprinted by permission.
>
> page 78, negative number F-5441 10025494, O. T. Davis, reprinted by permission.

Denver Public Library, Western History Collection:

> page xvii, negative number F11426, reprinted by permission.
>
> page xx, negative number F36791, reprinted by permission.
>
> page xxi, negative number X13690, reprinted by permission.
>
> page 14, negative number F27497, reprinted by permission.
>
> page 15, negative number F12882, reprinted by permission.
>
> page 17, top, negative number F19144, R.R. Doubleday, reprinted by permission.
>
> page 17, bottom, negative number F19139, reprinted by permission.
>
> page 36, negative number F30302, reprinted by permission.
>
> page 51, negative number F18425, reprinted by permission.
>
> page 68, negative number F8139, Dagleish, reprinted by permission.
>
> page 69, negative number F25786, reprinted by permission.
>
> page 75, negative number F26479, Walker, reprinted by permission.
>
> page 77, negative number X21934, reprinted by permission.
>
> page 79, negative number NS537, Salsbury, reprinted by permission.
>
> page 80, negative number F19138, reprinted by permission.
>
> page 83, negative number F22779, reprinted by permission.
>
> page 84, negative number F27407, reprinted by permission.
>
> page 85, negative number Z629, Holland, reprinted by permission.
>
> page 105, negative number NS-15, Holland, reprinted by permission.
>
> page 106, negative number X21560, reprinted by permission.
>
> page 109, negative number Z-147, reprinted by permission.
>
> page 110, negative number Z-330, reprinted by permission.
>
> page 111, negative number X22141, reprinted by permission.
>
> page 112, negative number X22165, reprinted by permission.
>
> page 114, negative number NS-124, Salsbury, reprinted by permission.
>
> page 125, negative number X14731, reprinted by permission.

Library of Congress, Prints and Photograph Division, John C. Grabill Collection, LC-: page xxii, USZ62-13227, reprinted by permission.

Nebraska State Historical Society, Solomon D. Butcher Collection: page 76, collection number R62608, item number 2167A, reprinted by permission.

The Frederic Remington illustrations, pages 13, 57, and 61, reprinted from *Ready-to-Use Old West Cuts*. Dover Publications, 1995.

The bucking bronco graphics reprinted from *Ready-to-Use Old West Cuts*. Dover Publications, 1995.

The illustrations on pages xix, 73, and 123, reprinted from *The American West in the Nineteenth Century: 255 Illustrations from "Harper's Weekly" and Other Contemporary Sources*. Dover Publications, 1992.

The map on page 6, from *Cowboy Culture*, by David Dary, copyright 1981 by David Dary. Used by permission of Alfred A. Knopf/Random House.

The José Cisneros illustrations, pages 5, 7, 9, and 32, from *Riders Across the Centuries: Horseman of the Spanish Borderlands*, by John O. West and José Cisneros, Texas Western Press, 1984. Used by permission of Texas Western Press.

The José Navaro brand on page 59 reprinted by permission of David McDonald, Casa Navarro State Historical Park, San Antonio, Texas.

The Spanish brands on page 60 from *Los Mesteños: Spanish Ranching in Texas, 1721–1821* by Jack Jackman, Texas A&M University Press, 1986, reprinted by permission.

Gene Autry's Cowboy Code, page 117, used by permission of the Autry Qualified Interest Trust, copyright 1994.

The Hopalong Cassidy Creed, page 117, reprinted by permission of U.S. Television Office, Inc.

The Roy Rogers Rider Club Rules, page 118, reprinted courtesy of the Roy Rogers–Dale Evans Museum.

The cowboy sayings on pages 100–103 from *How to Talk Cowboy: Sayings of the Old West*, by "The Old Wrangler." Reprinted by permission.

The childhood photograph on page xii courtesy of the author.

The original illustrations by Carol Kimball throughout this book are reprinted with her permission.

Index

About the Author

Photo credit: Jan Pelton

Angel Vigil is Chairman of the Fine and Performing Arts Department and Director of Drama at Colorado Academy in Denver, Colorado. He is an award-winning author, performer, stage director, and educator. As an arts administrator, he has developed many innovative educational arts programs for schools and art centers.

His awards include the Governor's Award for Excellence in Education, a Heritage Artist Award, a Master Artist Award and a COVisions Recognition Fellowship from the Colorado Council on the Arts, the Mayor's Individual Artist Fellowship, and a Theatre Educator of the Year Award from the Colorado State Theatre Association.

Vigil is the author of four books on Latino culture. His book *The Corn Woman: Stories and Legends from the Hispanic Southwest* was awarded the prestigious New York Public Library Book for the Teen Age National Award. His book *Una Linda Raza: Cultural and Artistic Traditions of the Hispanic Southwest* won the Border Regional Library Association Southwestern Book of the Year Award and the Colorado Book of the Year Special Recognition Award. His other books are *¡Teatro! Hispanic Plays for Young People*, and *The Eagle on the Cactus: Traditional Stories from Mexico*.

Vigil is an accomplished storyteller specializing in the traditional stories of the Hispanic Southwest and Mexico. He has performed at national storytelling festivals throughout the United States and is a featured storyteller on *Do Not Pass Me By: A Celebration of Colorado Folklife*, a folk arts collection produced by the Colorado Council on the Arts. He has also created an historical character performance for the Colorado Endowment of the Humanities: Diego Martín, *El Vaquero*, Stories of America's First Cowboy.